MW00572129

Conversion

FATHER DONALD HAGGERTY

Conversion

~

*Spiritual Insights into
an Essential Encounter
with God*

IGNATIUS PRESS   SAN FRANCISCO

Cover art: *The Calling of Saint Matthew*
Michelangelo Merisi da Caravaggio
S. Luigi dei Francesi, Rome, Italy
© Scala/Art Resource, New York

Cover design by Roxanne Mei Lum

© 2017 by Ignatius Press, San Francisco
All rights reserved
ISBN 978-1-62164-211-4 (PB)
ISBN 978-1-68149-777-8 (eBook)
Library of Congress Control Number 2017941802
Printed in the United States of America ♾

Sister M. Delphinus, M.C.

and

Sister M. Renato, M.C. (1969–2005)

Contents

Foreword

Though relatively brief in length, Father Donald Haggerty's *Conversion* offers an in-depth exploration into the spiritual/ascetical basis for serious growth in Christ. On every page, laymen and clergy alike are invited to draw closer to Jesus by dying to self in a lifelong series of "yeses" that yield an ongoing inner transformation or conversion experience. Father Haggerty's familiarity with the great conversion stories of our Catholic tradition—Saint Augustine, Saint Francis of Assisi, Saint Ignatius of Loyola—is evident, but it is his synthesis of their stories, developed throughout his twenty-five years as confessor, spiritual director, seminary formator, and retreat master that offers the serious reader penetrating and challenging insights into our spiritual journey.

Solid growth in the spiritual life is fleeting and illusory unless it is rooted and lived out in the suffering and death of Christ on the Cross. Thus, while God's lavish mercy is limitless, it does not come without the cost of permanent and painful changes in life. (Satan is at work in a "feel-good" faith that promises paradise to one and all without the struggle for radical conversion in our lives.) The role of the Blessed Mother in this process of converting souls for her Son is highlighted in rich detail in this book. Those who have known her loving and merciful intervention in their lives tend to become people who honor her desire that we seek souls for her Son.

In addressing the clergy, what the author calls "cerebral orthodoxy" and "bourgeois clerical life" is bravely exposed as a betrayal of the call to follow Christ in his invitation to "drink the chalice that I drink" and to renounce worldly attractions for the sake of the Kingdom. Likewise, for lay people, there are provocative reflections to ponder as the Lord is sought more fully after a conversion experience. Ordinary events in the life of every Christian are intimately involved in God's eternal design, a God who frequently uses unexpected events and unlikely encounters in bringing about the graces of conversion. (The converted soul often becomes the instrument used by God for the conversion of other souls.)

This is not a work for casual or light reading. It demands meditative moments, honest and prayerful self-reflection, and, most of all, a sincere desire to know Christ and his truth ever more deeply as we pursue the path toward the lofty goal of genuine gospel discipleship proposed by Father Haggerty. May this timely book be a means of grace in many lives.

Edwin F. Cardinal O'Brien
June 15, 2017
Solemnity of Corpus Christi

Introduction

Immediately before and for a good while after my conversion, I was of the opinion that to lead a religious life meant one had to give up all that was secular and to live totally immersed in thoughts of the Divine. But gradually I realized that something else is asked of us in this world and that, even in the contemplative life, one may not sever the connection with the world. I even believe that the deeper one is drawn into God, the more one must "go out of oneself", that is, one must go to the world in order to carry the divine life into it.

—Saint Edith Stein

At a side altar in the Church of San Luigi dei Francesi in Rome is a magnificent Caravaggio painting depicting the call of Saint Matthew the tax collector. A young rakish Matthew in his twenties sits slumped over a table surrounded by some friends and associates. His head is bent downward, and his eyes are downcast and staring. One hand dangles feebly near the scattered coins in front of him. Jesus stands a few feet before Matthew at the other side of the table, with a piercing gaze cast upon him. Behind Jesus, a strong beam of light shines into the room from the doorway. Jesus' arm is horizontally raised across the table, and a single finger of his outstretched hand points directly toward Matthew. The other figures in the scene are all aware that Matthew alone has been signaled. Matthew's discomfort, his desire to disappear with no place to hide, is all too clear. The painting captures wonderfully a man's soul confronting its hour of truth. Caravaggio takes us inside that long, dreadful instant of painful uncertainty when a decision must be made for or against Jesus Christ, the crossroad that will mark a lifetime depending on a soul's choice.

This centrality of conversion is striking throughout the four Gospels. There are a number of variations on the theme. The call to abandon a previous life, dropping everything at once to follow Our Lord on an itinerant, unknown journey, is the summons heard by Peter and Andrew, James and John, at the Sea of Galilee. A conversion in this case does not mean that a bad life has been left behind, a parting with evil ways. The conversion here involves a radical "yes" of personal fidelity to Jesus. The act overturns everything familiar and instantly attaches a life in a unique bond with Jesus Christ. The apostles all underwent such a conversion. The response did not make them immediate heroes or full of wisdom, zeal, and courage. It did place them for the next three years in constant proximity to Jesus. That closeness to him allowed the drawing power of his attraction to permeate their souls. Every person who goes far in a love for God and for souls will experience a similar pattern. The effect of following Our Lord after a very decisive choice for him, staying close to him especially in prayer, permits his presence to deepen its personal impact upon our life. A lifetime of spiritual need for God has its seeds in this initial period of conversion.

There are as well in the Gospels the conversions of more gravely sinful persons. The sinful woman described in Saint Luke's seventh chapter may have been Saint Mary Magdalen, who is mentioned by name in the next verses of chapter eight. In the home of a Pharisee, at a dinner party, this woman prostrates herself behind the feet of Jesus, pouring out her tears and perfume on the feet of Our Lord, kissing his feet and drying them with her hair. The Pharisee hosting this dinner is offended by the display and murmurs inwardly. Jesus already knows the repentance of this woman for her many sins. In fact, this hour may not be their first encounter. It is not inconceivable that she is the woman caught in adultery in John's eighth chapter whom he saved from stoning. Jesus' reply to Simon the Pharisee should be carved into every Christian heart. "Therefore, I tell you, her sins,

which were many, have been forgiven; hence she
has shown great love. (But the one to whom little is forgiven, loves little") (Lk 7:47; NRS). These
words are essential to every deeper understanding
of relations with God. Divine mercy is an extraordinary gift when great sins have marred a life. But
God's mercy is not intended simply for the forgiveness of sin. It is meant for the sake of a life
that will stretch ever farther after a conversion in
an intensity of love. The Lord who on an earlier
day rescued us deserves nothing less than a life of
great love in gratitude to him.

There is another type of conversion anticipated
in certain Gospel scenes, and this, too, is worthy of
our pondering. Jesus offers challenges in the Gospel
that will take time before they are understood in
their deeper significance. When James and John re-
quested seats on the right and left of Our Lord in
his kingdom, they were told that they did not know
what they were asking. "Are you able to drink the
chalice that I drink?" (Mk 10:38). This form of
conversion is always linked to some greater insight
into the Passion of Christ. We realize that the Passion of Christ has entered mysteriously into our
own life as a question—how far we are willing to
go in love for him? The admonition that we must
die to self for greater love is not just a spiritual
metaphor. In fact, it is a direct challenge issued on
the night before Jesus' own crucifixion. "Will you

lay down your life for me?" (Jn 13:38). To the degree we seek God with more intense love, we are on a path of confrontation with this question of dying for love of Christ. At some point long after an initial conversion, another leap of soul is necessary. A decisive "yes" to Our Lord is demanded, as it was earlier in life, but from a deeper layer of soul, overcoming any barrier of hesitation. Spiritual conversions of this kind may be the most important acts in our life. Crossing a threshold to an interior offering of all to God can lead to the gift of our entire life to him. Every saint in the course of a life underwent conversions of this type.

This book offers reflective insights on the experience of conversion and, in particular, on matters of spiritual importance that arise in the wake of a conversion. The aftermath of a conversion is as significant as the conversion itself. The soul's response to grace in this period after a conversion has a crucial impact on later life. It is one thing to be a prodigal son who returns to his father after coming to his senses and repenting. It is another thing to open one's eyes fully to the new life that beckons in the glowing sunrise of a recent conversion. The recovery of grace is always only a first step toward a discovery of immense possibilities in a life with God. This book takes up many points of interest calling for recognition after a conversion. The desire is to enhance an appreciation for

the graces and challenges that ensue after a conversion. A kind of contemplative reflection on these
issues can offer meditative thought for prayer and
further pondering. God is at work mysteriously in
souls that have returned to him. The effort here is
to delve into this mystery of the soul encountering
God in the experience of a conversion.

The book is organized as a collection of concise
observations concerned with matters that might
not be commonly pondered. The effort is to target
issues that may confuse us after a conversion or call
for some clearer understanding. There are obsta-
cles and challenges to be met as well as insights
to be cultivated after a conversion. For one thing,
spiritual sensitivity can be magnified when a soul
has been away from grace for a time. Reactions
can be strong, even exaggerated. New insights are
common, but they also demand proper interpretation. There are also providential interventions by
God in the time after a conversion that call for
careful attention. An entire life may be at stake.
Recognizing God's desires and his will is a crucial
task in this period and usually requires some assis-
tance. Sin is a reality that requires a more penetrating awareness after a conversion. Likewise, the
mercy of God can be more deeply honored after
a conversion precisely by understanding its true
nature. Other parts of the book expose symptoms
of grace that ought to be encouraged after a con-

version, such as a love for the Eucharist and the poor and a desire for simpler life-style and a kind of missionary zeal that awakens for souls and their salvation. A chapter on the conversion of priests is included as perhaps of particular value in the current day.

The most important section in this book concerns the possibility of a "second conversion" in the spiritual life. As the comments in this chapter observe, the call to holiness requires a second great awakening in our lives. Every conversion earlier in life is meant to proceed in the direction of a subsequent, deeper surrender to God. The third type of conversion mentioned above from the Gospels awaits every soul serious about God. But it is a conversion that demands a conscious interior choice on our part, a defining choice in prayer that takes us across a threshold of surrender to God. A passion for God begins then to burn in a life in a manner beyond any previous need for God. The result is the experience of new challenges in relations with God. The last chapter will address some of these repercussions. In short, we are capable of going far in our lifelong relationship with Our Lord once we penetrate more deeply the personal encounter God offers us in a conversion experience. The earlier conversions in our life arrive at their proper finality only when we allow God to invite us to a greater conversion of soul later in life.

Lastly, we might mention at the outset that great works in the Catholic tradition have recounted the stories of personal conversion. Saint Augustine's *Confessions* is the classic example, but the *Life of Saint Anthony of the Desert* from this ancient period can also be recalled. The biographies of saints such as Saint Francis of Assisi, Saint Ignatius of Loyola, or Blessed Charles de Foucauld are notable in the drama of conversion that transformed these lives. So-called "second" conversions are likewise part of the history of saints. The conversion described by Saint Teresa of Avila in her autobiography from religious laxity and mediocrity to a mystical life in the convent is a striking example. The stories of saints who converted to the Catholic faith such as Blessed John Henry Newman or the philosopher and Auschwitz martyr Saint Edith Stein, who read the autobiography of Saint Teresa in a single night and soon after sought entry into the Church, are equally fascinating. Reading a saint's biography or watching a film of a saint's life after reading this book might enhance our own spiritual desire for the deeper offering of ourselves to God.

Conversion - deepest spiritual beliefs

Preliminary Thoughts on Conversion

Although I abandoned you, Lord, you did not abandon me so completely as not to turn to raise me up by always holding out your hand to me. And often times, Lord, I did not want it; nor did I desire to understand how often you called me again.

—Saint Teresa of Avila

We live in the midst of so much danger and find it so hard to arrive at truth. The clearest and truest things are the darkest and most dubious to us, and consequently we flee from what most suits us.

—Saint John of the Cross

Fear not that thy life shall come to an end, but rather fear that it shall never have a beginning.

—Blessed John Henry Newman

At the heart of every conversion is an encounter with the mystery of God himself. We come to know that God is utterly personal and real in his mystery, with eyes of a secret penetration cast upon our soul. In a unique way for each person, he enters within our life to invite us to fix our gaze in the direction of his approach. If we allow ourselves to be drawn and step closer, a brief unmasking may take place. We know him then indisputably as our Lord and our God. All our prior reflection about God may seem at that hour unfocused and superficial, a chasing after shadows. For we perceive now that he possesses an exquisite personal quality beyond any previous idea we may have had. The certainty in faith of his presence in near proximity to our soul leads quite spontaneously to the prostration of our spirit before him. Every dramatic discovery of God in a conversion provokes us to our knees, ready now to pray from a deeper layer of soul, drawn to prayer often for the first time in our life.

Conversion is the spark that allows a soul to catch fire with God. It strikes the flint and begins the early burning of a passion for God. It is the first leap of flame that can quickly become a fire lasting a lifetime. Conversions are necessary for deeper spirituality, as many saints can testify. It would seem that no one without an experience of a serious conversion will be taken to the more profound depths of a personal encounter with God or invited by grace into a contemplative life of prayer. This seems to be almost a private maxim of Our Lord with souls. He wants us to know the experience of being finally conquered and subdued in the presence of his love. For being vanquished by him is essential to all greater love for him. And then, once he is known, he wants us to taste a longing and a pure desire for himself. We do not have to be sullied with terrible corruption in our lives to need this experience of conversion. We simply have to be ignorant of Our Lord to some degree. The flame ignites all the same whether sins are small or great for one primary reason. Whenever an overpowering encounter with Jesus Christ on his Cross at Calvary pierces our soul, he draws the deeper desire of the heart, and a conversion is ready. The sight of Jesus Christ crucified gazing down on us in a single hour of our life is sufficient to change us forever. But we must choose to seek such an hour. We cross a threshold in spiritual perception in looking at the eyes of this crucified man who is God himself, perhaps overcome by incomprehension of what he may be asking of us in his suffering.

~

A conversion is never planned or conceived as a personal project. It is not a prepared item on a life's journey. It may have a time of gestation, but that is difficult to measure. Most souls have no realization until they are near the event itself that they are moving in the direction of a conversion. It is not something ordinarily sought but, rather, seems to seek out a soul. The favor and predilection of God are always behind it. It is as though his eyes linger on certain souls, watching them for a time, before targeting them as a prey of his love. In truth, therefore, conversions are never entirely sudden, coming out of nowhere, even when they seem to ignite an explosively new force within a life. The hidden chiseling of the hand of God has usually been at work for an unknown time; concealed touches have been laid upon the heart; the trailing of the soul has taken place into its shadowed hours, sometimes for long periods of time, even for years. All these preliminary anticipations only point to the essential truth of a serious conversion. God meets a soul at a crossroad of life and in some unexpected way makes his real presence known. A personal encounter with the real mystery of a personal God is at the heart of every great conversion.

~

As much as God may draw a soul, leading it to the day of recognition that he desires, it remains for a soul to choose. God never exercises a last compelling push or shove across the threshold that finally takes a soul to its knees in a surrender of itself to God. There is always an interior act of consent to God that must be exercised deep in the soul, an utterly personal choice. The choice for God, with all its unknown risk and its uncertainty, takes our soul across the threshold of a conversion. This never happens except when an hour of decisive consent to God occurs, sometimes to the point of sweat and tears. Ordinarily the interior act in affirming a "yes" to God is accompanied as well by a visible action. The decision to seek a confessional when there is the long burden of sin, the choice to make an act of profound offering in the life of personal prayer, even a promise or vow, the decision to enter a monastery or cloister, a seminary or religious house—in each case a consent and personal surrender take place. The impact of that choice, which could have been refused, affects all that follows in our life. This personal choice and the determination it elicits from our soul can mark an entire life. Many souls become great spiritually because this first taste of a serious choice for God is never forgotten during their lifetime. Even in later struggles and in the shadowed periods of life, the capacity for a serious inward choice for God remains ready to be exercised once again. Their "yes" to God at the time of their conversion deepens into a "yes" to everything he asks over the course of their lives. The ability to find that "yes" many times again in a life shapes over time our relationship with God.

~

Saint Teresa of Avila makes an interesting comment when she writes of her admiration for the determination that Saint Peter showed in stepping out of the boat onto water at the invitation of Our Lord. The event is described in Saint Matthew's fourteenth chapter. Even in faltering a moment later, overcome with fear as he began to sink, Peter displayed an initial courage that was important for his future. Her comment is that this determination to step forward blindly and in trust was a sign of a great capacity of soul. It was only a first step, true, and followed quickly by an embarrassing cry for help, but it was still a leap of great magnitude and significant for his soul's later courage. Serious conversions of a spiritual nature require a determination to leave behind safety and security and venture toward an unknown possibility in God's plan for our soul. A step must be decisive, taken without calculating risks, simply because the voice of Our Lord invites us in some mysterious way. The summons to come must be all that is heard in that moment.

~

Our soul enters into an initial condition of vulnerability with every serious conversion. It is open now to being challenged and provoked, jabbed at and bruised, because something very personal has happened within the inward experience of the soul.

A serious conversion affects not simply the visible realm of a changed life-style, the cessation of unhealthy actions. It cuts inside to the depths and leaves its mark in the cracks and crevices of our inner soul. A discomfort is inevitable in every conversion because some emptying takes place in the depth of our soul. There is never an immediate replacement all at once of worldly desire with fervor for God. And so our soul is vulnerable in the early period after a conversion. The desire for Our Lord is just awakening, but it has not ripened adequately. A restless need for God may be felt, and there is often nothing to assuage it. Prayer itself may not satisfy the spiritual need we feel because we have not learned yet to pray more seriously. We learn at that time a first lesson that prayer is not like eating to relieve hunger. The hunger of our soul does not disappear with prayer; on the contrary, it often increases painfully with more prayer. It is the vulnerability of love that begins to be tasted in the early experience of prayer after a conversion.

~

When we reflect back on a conversion, we may realize that it is to brush up against a secret in God, to sense a veil somewhat lifted, as though a quality of shyness in God is suddenly perceived that was never considered before. A taste of this exquisitely

personal truth in God takes place. He is not hiding
in majestic distance; rather, he has become the Lord
Jesus of flesh and blood whose eyes respond to our
own glance. We can sense his lingering gaze and
his delight in returning our soul to his protection
and care. The secret disclosure he offers us, which
is only a taste at first, is the concealed wonder of his
wounds. The summons by Jesus to Saint Thomas
the Apostle after the Resurrection to place his finger in the nail marks and his hand in his side is repeated again in conversions. Our Lord wants this
probing, this sustained gaze and inquiry, a sifting
by intimate desire of his own disguised hiddenness.
The wounds remain in the body of Christ so that
a wound of love may persist in the soul that gazes
on them. It is as though Our Lord has been shy
to let these wounds be seen until a conversion has
taken place. And now, with our soul conquered by
him, he shares his secret. The wounds of Our Lord
become for our soul a never fully fathomed reality
in the mystery of relations with him. They always
invite further probing and contemplation that can
seem endless as our life continues. "Look at my
wounds and contemplate them in love", he seems
to say. The secrecy of God in this mystery of his
wounded love opens itself more with each entry of
our soul into the depth of his thirst for souls. The
depth is limitless, and always, after a conversion, it

is this truth of his heart full of infinite desire and wounded in love that awaits our discovery.

∼

Shortly after World War II, in Paris, a thirteen-year-old Jewish boy who had survived the German occupation while losing his parents to the concentration camps entered the Cathedral of Notre Dame along with two Catholic friends of the same age. They were in a mischievous mood, and the two Catholic boys dared the Jewish boy to enter the confessional and pretend to make a confession to the priest. They wrote down some necessary words and gave him a quick instruction on the usual procedure. The Jewish boy took up the challenge and disappeared into the confessional. Apparently he lacked sufficient dramatic skills to fool the priest, who presumably did not give him the Church's sacramental absolution. Nonetheless, at the end of the confession, the priest did give him a penance. He was told to walk across the cathedral to the adjacent far side, and there he would find a very large crucifix and a man nailed to it. There he was to kneel down and to look carefully in the face of that man on the Cross and then slowly to say ten times in a whisper, "I do not care what you suffered for me on that Cross." The Jewish boy was unable to get past the seventh repetition of these whispered words. By that time he was in tears and had realized in faith the Christian truth that he was looking at an image of God himself hanging on a Cross.

~

Not long after a serious conversion, it happens that the immense distance between goodness and evil can become very lucid to our awareness. There is an intuition of soul that there is no middle ground between the two, no overlap or sharing, and that a choice in life is inevitably made for one or the other. Before that point in time, the line between good and evil may have been blurred. No keen sight existed within us for the strict demarcation and barrier dividing good and evil. Perhaps only rarely did we think our personal choices to be actually evil or considered the possibility of casting ourselves into the party of the devil. Now, after a conversion, we may recognize the ominous path we were walking, and the result is a kind of moral clarity of soul. A sense of the horror of insulting God, of the arrogance of sinful rebellion, and of painful hurt to others all come to the fore. The regret for the past brings a salutary awareness. It causes sensitivity to the true danger of a choice against God. And that same awareness prepares our soul for a deeper understanding of the greatness in choosing to give ourselves fully to goodness and to God.

~

It is a reality as well in conversions, even when they are most lasting and sharp in their intuitive awakening, that a shadow side of the soul remains still alive and, indeed, never dies. In that sense, a conversion cannot be compared to the elimination of a foreign menace from the soul, like the removal of cancer from the body. A conversion may entail a soul's return to the state of grace with a sacramental confession of serious sins. But even then the significance is less the expunging of sin and much more the entry of God into the deeper hunger of the soul. This gift of God to the soul, however, does not prevent the possibility of turning back and reversing direction. The burden of a human vulnerability to sin remains. It is mysterious and vexing that nothing is ever completely secure in the relations with God. Throughout our life, our soul's choice for God has to be continually renewed and deepened with the help of grace. Unfortunately, there are many examples of souls who have great conversions and exercise fervent love for God for some years and who nonetheless falter at a point later in life and lose everything. There is hardly a priest or religious in today's Church who cannot recount personal contact with sad instances of this truth.

~

It ought to be said, too, that a conversion does not make life entirely easier. It often brings as well the first bitter taste of emptiness in worldly pursuit. Conversions do not of course incapacitate or strip a person of worldly ability, but they often have the effect of undermining our ambitions in life. With the experience of God in some mysterious manner, we get a taste of eternity without quite knowing what we are experiencing. In a brief instant, there is a change in perception, and we begin to sense a purpose in life that extends beyond this life itself. The passing nature of everything in life may crystallize in an intuition ever so briefly and permanently enter our soul's awareness. We suddenly see differently, not as though everything has turned upside down, but rather with a certain wisdom now penetrating our vision. The distant perspective comes into focus; the experience of time changes. We may begin to view our life in some sense as an exile and a waiting, a pilgrimage toward an ultimate destination that awaits us. This mild taste of eternity as a greater truth than passing time reduces to some degree our attraction for the passing things of life. Only the most significant

realities seem worth the expenditure of our passion
—family, our Catholic faith, God himself. The experience is often felt as an open invitation to make
prayer an essential hunger in our life. We may discover that prayer is in itself a kind of perpetual
waiting for the veil of eternity to be lifted.

~

A serious conversion is never a personal accomplishment, an achievement that we might savor
with some satisfaction. In a very pure sense, it is entirely a gift of God when a soul returns to a friendship with him or discovers his real presence for the
first time in life. But there is another truth behind
conversions that is often less noted. It may also be
that the Virgin Mary always has her eyes on a soul
that undergoes any form of conversion. She is the
mother of conversions and often in a very direct
manner. She asked Saint Bernadette many times in
the apparitions at Lourdes to pray for the conversion of sinners. Bernadette recounts that each time
Mary made this request, the young seer asked Our
Lady what she meant by these words. And each
time, in reply, Mary only smiled at her. There is a
mystery in that smile of Mary. Did she smile at the
zeal of Bernadette's desire to get it right and fulfill
the request properly? Or perhaps Mary smiled in
knowing already that this girl in the years to come

would offer much in sacrifice and self-giving for the conversions of many souls. As in all the apparitions of Our Lady, the passage reminds us that conversions occur because prayer and sacrifice have been placed in the heart of Mary for the sake of souls. The personal experience we might have in every serious conversion of being drawn to Our Lord has hidden within it the presence of Mary and these intercessions. Mary wanting a soul for her Son because her own love for that soul is strong is one reason behind every conversion.

~

In the Bronx, New York, where I was working as a lay volunteer some years ago with the Missionaries of Charity in their men's shelter, one Sister made fully evident to me Mary's involvement in conversions. After we met, this Sister began to prod and dig at my soul with a repeated line of questioning. Initially it seemed merely an interest in my life and what I might be seeking. But she had no vocation for diplomatic subtleties, and soon she was affirming with conviction that I had a vocation to the priesthood and should wake up to the truth. I put her off politely for a time, but she persisted in turning every conversation toward this matter of the priesthood. "It is between God and my soul," I said, "let him and me decide." But her retort invariably consisted of a dismissive shake of the head and an insistence that I would see. One day, perhaps losing her patience, she said she was going to pray a novena to the Virgin Mary for this intention. The fifth day of that novena, a different Sister asked another volunteer and myself to come to the convent after Mass to do a small job. The wooden trim on the edge of the convent's front door had loosened and needed to be hammered back in. I began to hammer vigorously and was on the third nail when I was hit hard on the head by something. The blow almost knocked me to the ground. As I bent over, the blood was trickling freely to the pavement. The doorbell was rung, but before we entered the convent, the mystery of this collision was made known. A large and rather heavy statue of the Virgin Mary, formerly lodged on a pedestal overhanging the front door of the convent, had taken a fall with the vibrations of the hammering and had managed to land quite flush on the crown of my head. After a few minutes, the Sister interested in my conversion entered the room where a white towel now full of blood lay over my head. When she inquired a bit anxiously what had happened and heard "the Blessed Mother dropped on his head" and then saw the statue lying on the table, her face changed. The comment was swift and clearly relished—"Thank God, I hope maybe now you will wake up." And like many nuns I have come to know, she was exactly right.

~

Finally, we should say, a serious conversion draws a soul to prayer, if only we can recognize this attraction. At the time of a conversion, the first deeper hungers for God are felt for the mystery of God, and the result can be a quiet urgency to seek time in prayer alone with him. A need takes hold in the soul to unfold the layers of silent mystery that wrap around the presence of God. Often the thought of God may return, and we want more and more to taste of his presence. Prayer itself in this early period after a conversion is often a privileged time. The presence of God seems alive and vivid when we turn to prayer. And the newly converted soul may share in some of the same inclinations that a soul long practiced in the life of prayer experiences. The desire is strong to remain simply quiet in God's presence, for instance, speaking very little, savoring the sense of blessing. The words of Our Lord in the Gospel may leap into the heart with poignancy. The sense of God's presence and his gaze on the soul can be strong and undeniable. In truth, the soul is being favored in this hour of life. If prayer continues to be sought and silence becomes a sacred portion of each day, our soul may discover far more in God than could ever be anticipated, and trials may well be included in these relations with God. Every experience of conversion therefore raises an essential question: Will we now seek him in prayer with ever-increasing hunger and need? If we do, our life will be entirely altered from what it might have been. The vast differences in souls may hide in our lived response to this question. It is above all the commitment to prayer that will determine the course of our life after a conversion.

2

Aftermath of a Conversion

You called, you shouted, and you broke through
my deafness. You flashed, you shone, and you dis-
pelled my blindness. . . . I have tasted you, now I
hunger and thirst for more. You touched me, and
I burned for your peace.

—Saint Augustine

Isn't it the greatest possible disaster, when you are
wrestling with God, not to be beaten?

—Simone Weil

The more I gave up, the more happiness I found.

—Charles de Foucauld

*The period of time after a conversion is often decisive for
a lifetime. It is a privileged interval of discovery, not just
in coming to know God more vividly, but in sensing a request from God to let our life be used by him. The ex-
plosive force of grace experienced in a conversion lingers in
its effects and often casts a sharp light on God's desires for
the steps he wants us to take now in life. He has revealed*

his presence in a personal manner, and now he begins to
reveal a purpose in our life that was never previously sus-
pected. At the same time, this light may not answer all
questions. We may know with certainty after a conversion
that we belong to God in a special manner. But we may
not have concrete answers about how this belonging to God
affects the significant choices in our life. Nonetheless, the
graces are real in which God is drawing the soul to desire
a life deeply rooted in him. He wants our life offered to
him only from a free desire animated by love. Converted
souls sometimes become saintly souls because they leap in
that decisive time of grace toward the vista of a great gift of
themselves to God.

A man who has lost his faith in God will ordinarily
hide from the deeper loneliness of soul that accompanies his time of unbelief. He is loath to face his
real aloneness and inner absence. But if he recovers his religious faith, it is impossible to ignore the
change within his soul. No more does he feel as if
trapped in a closed room of senseless partitions and
blocked entryways, looking for exits and finding
none. A door has opened, a release has taken place.
Perhaps no one in that new state of soul can say
whether he has escaped a confinement or if someone else has entered and ended his isolation. What
is known is that his soul is no longer *alone.* Companionship with God can seem a simple occurrence
in those days and an easy delight. And there can

be a naïve expectation that the friendship is only beginning and will be permanently enjoyed in this manner. But the gift is temporary, an interlude before the real friendship begins. In time a new experience of solitude introduces itself, a different loneliness that has changed along with the change in the soul. A man comes to know it in seeking a Lord who hides himself more often and in waiting for his return in prayer, a wait that may stretch at times beyond days and weeks. Once, however, the waiting and the loneliness are understood as a new form of gift, a hunger for God can commence that has no limit over a lifetime. If a man is faithful to returning to it and does not fear it, nothing in this life can diminish that hunger and nothing can replace it.

~

Getting trapped and mired in serious sin for an extended time is for some people never separated from a need, after a serious conversion, to give their life completely to God. Conversions in these lives do not just provide some restoration to normality. The sins of the past do not recede into vague, distant memories. In these people, a conversion retains a youthful presence, even after long years, a never exhausted urging felt in the soul to give continually more to God. From the outside, perhaps, it might look as though a reaction to guilt drives such lives. But the psychological interpretation neglects the more interesting truth. In every age, there are souls whose desire for God is intense *because of* their previous sins. The years they lived forsaking God accentuate the shock of his rescue. What follows is lifelong astonishment at God's mercy, as if he loved in this manner only in rare instances, and they have been so favored. Divine mercy remains for them a first love, never abandoned, and this love affects everything in their subsequent lives. Not surprisingly, many of these souls follow a road that takes them increasingly toward deeper prayer. And their prayer has a common quality no matter what their external lives display. They learn soon to pray with great charity in intercession for souls like themselves who need also to receive the anonymous favor of a silent benefactor's pleading for a soul's conversion.

~

In some lives, forgiveness from God becomes an invitation to dismiss the past as a bad nightmare, irrelevant to a current life. But the past does not disappear so easily, nor should it. It lingers even after forgiveness, and perhaps with a definite purpose, for a true conversion does not signify simply a withdrawal from sin. It introduces for a time a chance for a new discovery, and in great sinners this can be a profound realization. Desires for an absolute purity and generosity awaken sometimes at the edge of what could have been a ruined life, precisely where we would not expect this form of desire. Recognition that lost periods of a life can never be returned can provoke an intense desire to give completely to God what is yet remaining in a life. The soul scarred by former sin is sometimes, after grace, the soul that will give without reserve. It is not at all an exaggeration to affirm that great sinners often do become hidden saints.

~

Toward the close of the Spanish Civil War, two soldiers from the Communist Republican faction were returning to their barracks after a night of drinking and cavorting with prostitutes. They were walking down a dusty road not far from a Carthusian monastery when the bells of the monastery began chiming loudly in the early morning light. With the bells ringing, their conversation halted, and they walked on in silence. The war ended not long after, and first one, then the other, joined this monastery. Around 1961, a newly ordained auxiliary bishop, later to become Cardinal Archbishop of Madrid, paid a visit to the monastery, hoping to meet these men and hear their story. He had heard on a number of occasions about their conversions and their entry into the monastery. He was received into the monastery by the abbot, and they took a slow walk through the corridors and grounds of the monastery. The bishop was waiting for a chance to ask if these men were still there. When he inquired, the abbot nodded and guided him outside. They entered the Carthusian grave-yard, where among the simple white crosses the ab-bot stopped in front of a grave, silent for a while, brushing the loose dirt with the toe of his san-dal. "This is one of them", said the abbot. "And the other?" Looking up now into the face of the bishop, the abbot replied, "I am the other."

~

After a serious conversion, strangely enough, the entire past can become sacred, including the times of great sin. Not that these sins are falsely honored or lifted up for show with a pretense of bravado and vanity. Something more spiritually rich can occur. Even the most regrettable deeds can become part of a blessed recollection, at least to some extent. Of course they are not fond memories, nor are they items for nostalgia. At the same time there is no need to turn back repeatedly in shame. To scour and scrape away at memories would be to forget that God was always present even when he was far from our mind and we seemed most eager for our own destruction. The great insight in looking back upon past sin is to realize that God did not descend out of nowhere upon the hour of conversion. He was an unrecognized companion even while we walked the dark path. Many times he gave quiet hints of himself, which we did not see. Often he was reaching out a hand of protection even when we had no sense of a protector close by. We might not have survived in life otherwise. He was never far behind our back, even as we turned it to him in those days.

~

For all the drama and protracted struggle that often accompany a serious conversion, the soul may be only briefly flooded with peace. Everything is not at all so settled and secure. Especially in a young man or woman who has open options, a return to grace raises more questions, provokes further, unresolved yearnings. A deeper, unknown reality in life now beckons with unexplored promise. The prospect of experiencing God at a greater depth of intimacy is likely soon to seize the soul. At first it is hardly felt, and even ignored, but the repetition of this offer can pulse with insistence, at least for a period of time. It would seem that God exercises a pattern with souls during this interlude. For along with the invitation to seek him and to taste his truth in a personal way, God seems to pose a more radical and distressing question. This question cannot be trifled with or delayed for too long without a loss. Soon it may no longer disturb the soul, and something irrecoverable can be squandered. A

sacred possibility burns in these days that a soul
may not realize sufficiently . . . *to belong completely
to God? to give entirely to God?* Never are these words
shouted; never are they heard in a tone of forceful
command. Rather, a whisper speaks them gently
from a depth inside the soul. They demand attention and courage because the voice is soft. It is a
quiet, delicate summons and, for that reason, easily
deflected or silenced. The risk is that the invitation
will fade without notice, disappearing beneath the
flow of life sweeping across the surface of days.
For a limited time, the need for recognition will
press upon the soul as though a kind of mysterious deadline is present. Yet a soul may not realize
it. An impulse of generosity must take place, the
awakening of a perception. Otherwise, the courage
for great things present for a time after a conversion will begin to dull. Giving oneself in a great
gift to God may soon seem a bizarre and quixotic
notion, the imaginings of a temporary delirium.
Caution and hesitancy and indecisiveness toward
God will intrude, a fear of unnamed costs in getting too close to God. It may not take long before
the attraction of a bold choice for God will drift
into forgetfulness. This of course does not mean
that a soul loses faith. What it does lose, and for
some souls not without a lifelong regret, is the fire
of a love and a longing for God that with one resolute leap might have become the great passion of
an entire life.

~

When the recovery of faith in God shakes a soul with a certain spiritual violence, two things in subsequent days are sometimes seen together—an intense desire for God and, more strangely, a hunger for exile from everything to that point familiar in a life. Why should they be so joined? The first is understandable; but why the attraction for leaving behind all that is familiar and that gives a personal life its identity? Why this desire to head off in a direction of risk and possible suffering? The symptoms of this pattern can be observed in numerous cases. There follows at times in lives an almost reckless unconcern for basic prudence. Talents become suddenly unimportant, ambitions are repudiated, education and experience are discounted, worldly pleasures are renounced. To an outsider, it seems an irrational state, an absence of sane, sensible reasonableness. Yet such souls, despite the murmurs and surrounding disapproval, have no personal sense of extremism. It is a great attraction they are following, and not primarily a spirit of radical renunciation. In a manner beyond the comprehension of friends and relatives, the prospect of a life filled with God magnetizes their hearts. It is not exile in itself that draws them; a deep desire for God burns within them and draws them. The possibility of a spiritual setting where they will become a stranger to the world, known in some secret manner only

to God, entices them as the only proper place in
life to give all to God. Who should say these desires are exotic or should doubt that they can be
sustained over a lifetime when in fact many souls
in history have found their happiness precisely in
giving themselves to the appeal of such yearnings?
In many souls hidden from the eyes of this world,
the mysterious grace of this pattern has played itself
out in ways the world will never know. The cloisters, the monasteries, the foreign missions trace the
evidence of this phenomenon in the shifting sands
of time. But one thing is certain. God himself is
surely the concealed companion within such longings, the partner in the secret of a great drama,
whispering of an immense happiness that is possible when a soul steps forward in the gamble of a
life given exclusively to God.

~

A suspicion that we are deceiving ourselves may accompany the early stage of a conversion. The experience is a doubt, not of God, but of ourselves,
and of whether presumption fuels our desire for
God. The thought of the great cost to self in religious pursuit harries us, and we may not feel strong
enough for it. We may feel unable to declare hon-
estly that we can accept a price still unknown to
us. There are many who after a conversion from

serious sin cannot read of Saint Peter's confident promise to Jesus at the Last Supper—"I will lay down my life for you" (Jn 13:37)—without wondering if, like Peter, three imminent denials await them in the near future. With that misgiving may come the concern that should a passion for God fade or prove impossible to sustain, or be lost by carelessness, an emptiness will take hold within the soul and trail the rest of a life. For it is clear now that no turning back is possible to a time in life when God was ignored and a carefree attitude was enjoyed. Once experienced deeply in faith, the discovery of God cannot be renounced in a manner that recovers an earlier absence of the thought of God. When God has become real for a soul, he cannot be simply forgotten, dropped and discarded, as one might toss a finished book in a dustbin. True, God can be rejected and a soul may lose faith again, but God cannot be simply forgotten once a genuine depth of faith has awakened in a soul. This truth has a further consequence, that happiness in any purely worldly pursuit is no longer possible. In some form or another after a serious conversion, a yearning for God will never disappear from a soul. A soul may betray this desire and even seek to crush it, but the desire does not die. And perhaps this is the reason for the initial anxiety of a soul concerning its perseverance in faith. It knows by a kind of spiritual instinct that it is now forever marked.

What it needs to realize by prayer is that this mark is also a seal of fidelity and promise from God. Nothing other than the soul's own rejection can keep God from returning repeatedly and remaining in pursuit of this soul. As the Gospel testifies, the three denials of Saint Peter did not end there. They were succeeded by an implacable divine pursuit and by the three questions of love directed to Peter by the resurrected Christ in the early morning light at the shore of the Sea of Galilee.

~

It happens sometimes, after a conversion, when all should be brisk movement under a light step, that a fatigue is felt, a heaviness and stiffness in stride. Time has passed, and the spiritual energy that galvanized the struggle against sin has subsided and settled down. The tedium of ordinary, uninspiring virtue has replaced the harder battle to overcome sin. Turning back to past sins may not be at this point a real threat. Instead, another form of testing takes place. A fear can arise of missing God's summons, his intervention and request for a decision, an important instruction he wants to impart. The possibility of neglecting some direction from God significant for the future begins to afflict our soul. The sense that a clue or quiet hint is being prepared and must be recognized makes our soul anxious. The thought that an unknown personal decision is looming becomes a recurring distraction. The desire to know what God wants from us can be urgent. A delay might be harmful; the loss, irrecoverable. All this worry and anxiety, however, may be misguided and without reason. God may not be asking for a particular decision of any kind at that hour. It is true that he does not permit complacency about the future, as though the days ahead require no seeking and will take care of themselves. But surely he intends to lead us to his desires. On the other hand, perhaps the anxiety has the useful purpose of carving a need to recognize a deeper offering that still awaits our life. The desire for that offering must become a permanent and prodding hunger in our soul. This desire for a deeper offering to God, if once it is embraced as an indispensable element of prayer, is often a first step in taking any soul into the graces of a contemplative life. And for this reason God allows us to taste an inexplicable dissatisfaction and uncertainty about our life. His intention is not for us to look to external solutions. He wants us to open the eyes of our soul to something far more profound in prayer than we have considered as yet.

$\sim$

Every converted soul should take note of Saint John of the Cross' insight that memory is purified by the virtue of hope. Certainly past events do not change, including our sins. There is a fixed, factual truth to everything that has happened, an irrecoverable character to earlier choices, and effects that may be still consequential. Memory cannot alter that. In this sense, the past cannot be taken back. We may regret sin and repent, but events do not evaporate and disappear, and sometimes the memory of them causes disturbance. Yet the virtue of hope, rather than dimming memory, can cause a different kind of remembrance. Looking back at sin, we can perceive what we had not realized in the past: that God in an utterly personal manner was present in a perseverance of love through that lost time, keeping pace with us even as we may have plunged recklessly into sin. He was preparing our rescue even while we were oblivious to his love. Perhaps there were many quiet approaches to our soul even unknown to us. He never renounced us, and he never cast us from his gaze. A form of purification affecting our memory allows us to perceive that this faithfulness of God invites us to a conviction of hope for the rest of our life. A thread of continuity persists through past and present and future. For God, all is of one piece, united in the single gaze he casts on our life. God's perseverance in a work of mercy will be consistent with all his past faithfulness to our soul. The fidelity he has already shown us continues always. This recognition is indeed an essential certitude in every life that becomes prayerful and contemplative.

~

Supernatural hope forges an inexplicable sense of enormous trust in God that no logical train of thought can elicit. For in the perspective of divine providence and of God's love for souls, all is open to possibility, nothing is closed or determined, and God is swift to repeat after every misfortune that he is not deterred by human mistakes. Hope not only makes all things possible, but grants a vivid sense of the realistic likelihood that God will indeed accomplish all things that he desires. And what he desires above all to complete is the surrender of our life to himself. A soul might think it is simply exalted in optimism when it glimpses the fiery horizon of a great offering that awaits it if only it can keep moving on. In fact, it is filled with the grace of an expectation rooted in God himself. In stark contrast, hope is violated whenever we expect nothing more after a conversion than ordinariness in the life of faith, without any greater entry into the mystery of the divine presence as our life continues. When a conversion has not cut to the core of the soul, that is to say, when a soul has not yet experienced more deeply the desire after a conversion to offer itself fully and without reserve to God, it is in part because a soul has not arrived at a sufficient exercise of hope. Hope joined together with gratitude lifts the eyes of the soul in anticipation that there is much yet to see and hear from God. The Gospel itself testifies that God intends to reveal himself to every soul that belongs wholly to him. The hope of this possibility is not quixotic; it must be embraced with the absolute conviction of faith. In the exercise of hope, our desire for God will expand and swell into a demand to surrender ourselves completely to his love and to his purposes.

3

The Understanding of Sin

It happened that one day entering the oratory I
saw a statue representing the wounded Christ. . . .
I felt so keenly how poorly I thank him for those
wounds that, it seems to me, my heart broke. . . .
I threw myself down before him with the greatest
outpouring of tears.

—Saint Teresa of Avila

We experience good only by doing it. We experience evil only by refusing to allow ourselves to do
it, or, if we do it, by repenting of it.

—Simone Weil

But none of the ransomed ever knew
    How deep were the waters crossed.

—Alfred Lord Tennyson

*In one sense, sin has no mystery to it, no appeal of wonder
to the intellect, nothing that invites a search for discovery.
It is the opposite of truth in this regard. But in another
sense, the wounded tendency of human nature due to the
effects of original sin remains a perpetual enigma in life*

*and an ongoing mysterious struggle that every life faces.
Conversions involve a repudiation of past sins and a desire to keep them in the past. But the past in this case invites as well a constant remembrance that God blessed our
lives in rescuing us from the disaster of serious sin. Many
saints spoke of themselves as great sinners. In part this was
a reference to their earlier days of indifference to God and
rebellion in sin. They never forgot that a gratuitous intervention from Our Lord saved their lives. But they also
understood, because of a conversion, the need for a great
dependency on God for everything good in their life.*

It is impossible to predict the permanence of a serious conversion at the time it takes place. But one
observation seems true. Conversions dangle on a
thin thread unless a soul perceives that a return
to sin remains an open, easy possibility. This may
be why conversions strong in emotion do not always prove lasting. Conversions full of emotion
are sometimes too confident of never falling again.
They are too sure of a strength that is more uncertain. The hour of sorrow and regret in these conversions seems so clearly averse to sin. But no person lives in an unchanging state of holy emotion.
Conversions that endure are different, in part because emotion plays a secondary role. These conversions show a more sober experience of divine
mercy. A different perception is stirred, one not
bound primarily to emotion. They retain a mem-

ory, not so much of personal tears, but of a tender, inexplicable gesture from God. The event that sweeps upon the inner life for these souls is fixed forever in their mind. For them it is as though Jesus himself bent down like the good Samaritan upon an injured man on a dusty road, pouring balm on bleeding wounds while asking nothing in return. His arrival when least expected shakes the soul with its favor. Lasting conversions from great sin retain this memory of a rescue and always have this trait in common: they do not forget the shock that God one day bent down into the dust to touch the hopeless ruin of their scarred lives. The memory is not forgotten. This strange gesture of divine love, without forewarning or notice, is never taken lightly. These souls do not forget, and they are not ungrateful. The memory remains alive and is often enough recalled. For the same humility of God recurs to some degree at all times when God approaches again in mercy. And these souls are grateful with an increasing intensity for this sacred first mercy and for saving a life from ruin.

~

Why is it sometimes said that Our Lord wants us to bring failure and sinfulness to him *as a gift*? At first the question seems absurd and incomprehensible in suggesting that sins can be a gift offered to

God. It appears a clear contradiction to the genuine
effort of proving our love for him by virtue and
generous self-giving. Yet many saints came to realize the importance of bringing the fullness of self as
a gift to the foot of the Cross, which must include
the truth of an ineradicable tendency to sinfulness
in our lives. When Saint Jerome after many years
finally completed his translation of the Bible into
Latin in Bethlehem, it was Christmas time and he
thought to make this work his gift to the Christ
Child on his birthday. In a vision, the Child Jesus
appeared to him and told him that he did not want
his translation as a birthday gift. Jerome was upset
and perplexed after so many years of hard work,
and he questioned: "Then what do you want?"
"Give me your sins, Jerome. I want you to give
me your sins as my gift."

～

If we wonder what bringing our sins as a gift can
mean, we have to enter into Our Lord's gaze on
souls. And we have to realize that Our Lord is not
alone in gazing on us. The adversary, the evil one,
does likewise. It is a primary effort of the devil to
accuse us of a perpetual unworthiness before God,
of unsuitability for any friendship with God. For
many people, great or small in their sins, this accusa-

tion is perhaps received at face value. The evidence of their sins is indisputable, and the conclusion is not argued. The sense of unworthiness is embraced as a truth without qualification. What follows for a soul is often some sense of remoteness from God, a lack of confidence, an unwillingness to draw closer because the door seems closed. Our Lord's effort in our regard is to conquer this lie. The devil in his legalistic mentality wants sins, small and great, to be treated by God as impediments to the heart of Christ. Our Lord refuses to accept this demand. He wants us to ignore the devil's accusation and approach him precisely as sinful and humbled and repentant, with a confidence that our sins do not chase him away in disgust. Bringing our sins to him *as a gift*, in that case, does not mean that our sins in themselves are a gift pleasing to him. That would suggest we should commit greater sins and so give a bigger gift. It means allowing Our Lord to do what he wants to do, namely, to conquer the devil's lie to souls. Jesus wants to love souls with a love that overwhelms sinfulness with goodness. But to realize this truth, we cannot withdraw from his gaze of love even as we are aware of failure. We are simply doing then what pleases him immensely. He wants to love intensely the soul unafraid to stand naked and in need at the foot of the Cross. All the more is this true when a soul is holy and is bringing the steady and depressing small failings of a life and yet is confident of a great love poured out from the Passion of Christ upon the soul.

~

It no doubt takes much time spent in the presence of the Passion of Christ before we realize that our sinfulness and failing are not impediments to his love. On the contrary, he seems to love more intensely the soul that struggles with its wounds of human weakness and yet continues to stare up at him on the Cross with eyes of need. There is really no other answer for us in facing the implacable persistence of our wounded humanity than to take a place at the foot of the Cross. The time spent there in prayer does not at all incline a man to indulge his sins or to excuse them or exonerate them as inevitable in his life. What it does more mysteriously is to instill a sacred awareness of a divine love that is tender and perpetual despite every recent experience of failing again in our human nature. The paradox is strong here. The smaller the sins that go unconquered, despite effort and struggle, the more deeply a sense of tenderness from God may be experienced.

~

After a certain point in life, if a soul has been seeking God with some passion, it cannot give up and withdraw from this pursuit without a deeper wound to itself from which it will not recover except by turning back in a much more zealous need for God. And perhaps this explains why God may permit at times, without much resistance on his part, the lapse and straying of souls. For the soul's recovery of a passion for God will not be simply a delight to the heart of God. It means almost always in a soul a more intensely passionate pursuit of God. And for this great possibility, contrary to our own thought, God may be willing to risk the destiny of a soul.

~

A persistent feeling of guilt for past failures even after repentance keeps some people permanently oppressed in soul, always drawing back at the marred look and disfigurement they see in their own faces. It cannot be a fruitful sorrow for sin when a soul never leaves a depressing remembrance of the past as though it still held the soul in chains. Divine mercy is not then known except as an abstraction. Perhaps this overly sensitive remembrance of past sin is a form of self-conscious unworthiness that appeals to certain souls. But it misses a truth about God and is an obstacle to serious relations with him. God certainly does not cling to the past, as souls at times do. He does not examine our past sins over and over again. On the contrary, he wants the remembrance of any former sin simply to compel our soul to a clear recognition of mercy. And that awareness is meant for one thing: to make our soul uniquely fortified for the effort of seeking the conversion of other souls in need.

~

We should distinguish regret for sin, which is often fleeting, from a sorrow that will not pass so easily. Mere regret for the offensiveness of sin typically disappears, and sometimes after a short time. Once the regret for sin is forgotten, a forbidden attraction can quickly recover its appeal. But the other more lasting sorrow comes from recognizing that we have inflicted a wound on someone who is our God. A deeper knowledge that we have wounded him does not fade easily but, rather, begins to occupy our soul and draw tears of recognition within our soul. Perhaps it is God who does not allow a release from this remembrance that we have caused pain to him by our sin. For a time this sorrow can be like an extended illness even after the soul has been restored to grace. But as it turns gradually into a wound of love and is no longer felt as a debility limiting God's love, it begins to bless the soul. It is not disfiguring, even as it is recalled. It is not oppressive and discouraging, even as it cuts to the heart. Perhaps without this wound searing the soul in a quiet manner, we would never advance far in love.

～

At times the grace of repentance is received, and a soul does not turn back to a sin. But it also happens that serious sin lingers for a lifetime before the grace of repentance completes its work. In these lives, we might be tempted to ask why God did not intervene earlier to halt the progressive descent into moral failure. The ruin of a life, the waste that becomes more apparent over time—why did God not stop the downfall before it exacted its full price? The answer may not be simply the theological truth of human freedom and its capacity for resisting grace. It may also be that in some lives God simply waits, remaining nearby and not interfering, refusing to extend an easy rescue, allowing a life to edge precipitously close to destroying itself, because it is only then, in a last state of dire affliction, that some souls will finally recognize the true face of God. Perhaps in God's plan, these souls are companions to the good thief at the crucifixion, who surely has seen a vast collection of kindred souls join him over time. In these lives, the long, stubborn sins are a preparation for the cry of distress that at last escapes the throats of these souls, sometimes in their last minutes. This is very different from ordinary repentance in most lives, but it is also too real to ignore. It reflects God's desire that some souls in eternity give witness to a truly incomprehensible mercy that he has granted many "lost souls" in every age. This thought naturally affects our time in prayer and our own desire to make intercession for such souls.

~

Which is more difficult to reverse, more imperious in its demands? Craven bodily addiction when pleasure is sought greedily? Or a descent into spiritual inertia and the loss of all fight and struggle in a soul? Often, in a deadly way, these two are joined together, forming a toxic mix. We say there are no irreversible states of soul. Yet souls do despair at times, acquiring sometimes what is almost a sensual taste for powerlessness in considering themselves beyond reprieve. But what is at times remarkable to observe is how unwilling God is to concede the finality of that conclusion.

~

Some souls in their lifetime somehow come to a point of feeling no sorrow for sin even while intuitively sensing that this means a loss of God. The disappearance of God occurs, not by a passionate struggle, but indirectly as the sense of guilt vanishes from their conscience. Other souls, trapped hopelessly in their sins, never abandon a recurring reproach toward themselves and a painful thought of God. While it may appear that they bear a terrible burden of guilt, it may be more true to say that their form of self-accusation gives evidence of a mysterious refusal by God to allow a soul a permanent escape from his love.

~

The tragic turn of a sad, wasted life down a path of ruin often occurs without momentous warning. And yet, looking back on it, there is likely to be an ill-fated choice, a decision that already has the mark of a mortal wound about to be inflicted. There is at the time no recognition of the dark path about to emerge, but looking back it is certainly there. Think, for instance, in some lives of the first taste, out of curiosity, of the velvet pleasure of narcotic use. No one intends addiction in the first inquisitive taste of drugs. A more foolhardy confidence in self is usually present. The devil is surely present as well, seducing pride and a rebellious instinct in a human nature. If God is merciful toward such ruined lives, perhaps it is because he turns his gaze eternally on the tragic failure of that hour in the presence of evil when all subsequent loss remained still undetermined.

~

If we are not careful, especially after any serious conversion, we may not recognize the lie being whispered from the appearance of goodness in our current actions. With a practice now of virtue and regularity in our lives, we may imagine that we have somehow become a superior creature, elevated beyond the common man. We can spend a lifetime succumbing to this temptation, giving the devil at least a bone upon which to gnaw and keeping him interested. All serious relations with God in prayer depend on the remembrance of our own nothingness without him. Unless humility is deeply sought in our prayer, we risk a spiritual life of imaginative illusions. Indeed, the great need in the years after a conversion is often to realize how slowly we are actually advancing in grace.

~

Sometimes when a conversion has not been understood deeply enough as a divine act of immense, gratuitous mercy, and not in any way a personal accomplishment, a person adopts a cavalier vanity about the excesses of earlier days of rebellion. The casual allusions of some people to great sinfulness in their past can acquire at times a tone of subtle conceit. Perhaps the hidden thought is that recounting a dramatic conversion gives a push to those still not awakened to grace. And, if so, it can be worth the personal witness in a public setting. On the other hand, anyone who has truly understood the actual reality of sin cannot boast of a former life of transgression any more than one can boast of badly wounding a beloved parent.

~

We might assume that a conversion from great sin restores a soul to full, immediate health, casting its former life behind permanently. But this is not what usually happens. The wound to a soul from an extended period of sin may remain long after a return to grace. The reason is that our sins, even when forgiven, leave scars upon our soul and psyche. Serious sin over a period of time absorbs our souls in a repetition of self-centered choices, often without much regret. While it is true that all our sins are forgiven with repentance and a sacramental confession, the long indulged orientation toward self is not miraculously healed by the absolution of a priest. Self-love does not die so quickly. It is not excised simply with the repentance of sins and a sincere confession. Long after the disappearance of particular sins in a life, a soul may still struggle with deep-seated tendencies of egoism and selfishness. They come, however, in a different guise. While the temptation to former sins may no longer trouble a life, the wounding effect of former sins is still felt. The interior egoism that accompanied serious sins of the past reaches down into deep layers within the soul. Even with the soul restored to grace, an egoistic tendency does not disappear in a flash. Egoism remains a concealed influence, a recurrent temptation to place the self at the center of interest. And so what often happens for a time, even while a person is growing in grace, is simply a change of expression in egoism. From more overt indulgence in sin, there may be instead some variation of a kind of spiritual egoism. A person does not pursue God and virtue with a pure intention, for example, but strives for attention, desires notice, expects to be praised and even thought holy. Strip the façade from the external appearance of virtue, and we find our soul still ensnared in an embarrassing self-absorption. It is a reminder that serious sin leaves stubborn wounds. Longer purification is required when longer periods of grave sin held our soul in grip. Conversions of this sort must of necessity carve an intense desire for self-forgetfulness and humble dependence on God into deep regions of our soul.

Every serious conversion brings the risk of a new temptation in its early days. A power of perception may seem to have been granted, exposing the spiritual mediocrity of other lives in a way that did not irritate us previously. Having left behind our own misery, we can be inclined to look disdainfully upon what seems to be carelessness and indifference to virtue in others. This is a symptom of ignorance: the illusion of separation from the less worthy who seem to pursue only a very routine spirituality. In fact, we have not had time yet to prove anything of our own spiritual character. We mistake an attraction for high ideals with the actual realization of a closer union with God. And we assume that others have simply forsaken the higher aspiration, when actually they may simply consider the smaller things riveting our attention as unworthy of an excessive attention. In other words, who can say what God sees? The newly converted are not inclined, however, to ask this question.

There is a mercy from God directed, not toward obvious sinfulness, but to vanquishing something else that resists truth, a more subtle obstacle. After some perseverance in striving for God, we may

seem to arrive at a goodness achieved by our own
efforts. Actually this is a deception and a serious
spiritual obstacle. We are nothing without God,
and any goodness that flows through our lives has
its source in his gracious favor. This second mercy
of God brings to a soul awareness of that truth. It
is recognition of a deep need for God, the need
of a beggar for a benefactor, a perpetual need that
humbles us in real dependency on God. It gives as
well the grace not to resent the condition of abase-
ment that accompanies this recognition, a condition that is so easily offensive to our pride without our realizing it. Once God offers this second
mercy, we can anticipate that he will let poverty
in our soul intensify, not allowing us any illusion
of accomplishment in a worldly sense. From that
point on, our soul's insufficiency without God becomes inseparable from every real contact with his
personal presence. A pattern can be expected to repeat itself in many variations: every encounter with
divine mercy is preceded and followed by deeper
poverty within our soul, which is always precisely
the path into the graces of a deeper prayer life.

~

It is almost always true that a second great mercy
must pass over us if we are to give ourselves fully to
God. Before that blessed hour arrives, there can be

many isolated experiences of divine mercy due to the human struggle with sin. Every life acquires to some extent an unfortunate education in transgression, and some lives in serious ways. Many come to know their own version of the prodigal son's conversion and personal journey back to God. But lives that experience such a conversion do not always embrace a permanent passion for God, and this is why a second great mercy must be received. This second mercy for the soul is unlike any previous experience of mercy. The need for it is more difficult to recognize. It lacks the drama of danger and the risk of ruin that provoked the earlier awareness. It is needed, not because serious sin overwhelms and threatens a life, but because a soul suddenly wakes up to the realization that it has little actual love for God. Either the soul allowed the beginnings of love to fade, or it never had much love at all. If there was a time in its life when a passion for God did burn within it, this passion may have disappeared quietly from the soul through some form of neglect. Ironically, it may be that a more authentic passion for God was indeed present when sin was still a menace. The struggle with sin, while it continued, made a relationship with God a fiery and heated uncertainty. But now the soul has settled down to conventional practices of religious obligation. Now that virtue seems relatively secure, there are empty ashes in a heart where once a flame burned.

The irony of this tepid state must be confronted. It is only then that the second wave of mercy may pass into the soul, reaching deeper regions of desire within it. The realization that God cannot be neglected, and must not for a day be forgotten, catches fire within the soul. This is the mercy, if accepted, that can draw forth great generosity from a life. Without that second mercy, a passionate pursuit of God over a lifetime ordinarily does not happen.

4

The Mercy of God

When we see what Christ did in his weakness, what can he not accomplish in his power?

—Saint Bonaventure

I was a sea of sins and iniquities before receiving God's favors. . . . The reason I would like this known is that one might have knowledge of the great power of God. May he be praised forever.

—Saint Teresa of Avila

The poorer we are, the greater is Jesus' thirst to give himself to us.

—M.-D. Philippe, O.P.

The encounter with a merciful God ought to mark our lives forever. Yet this attribute of God's mercy, always inseparable from his love for souls, is easily taken for granted, precisely because it is always available to souls. The true meaning of mercy is understood only when another link is present. The mercy of God cannot be separated from the suffering that Jesus Christ endured at Calvary. An

*enormous cost permeates the divine offer of mercy to souls.
That cost is not something we must pay, but it is something we should never forget. We are forgiven all the sins
for which we repent in a conversion, but this truth implies
our recognition that precisely these sins tore apart the body
of Christ on the Cross. The reception of mercy requires an
effort to gaze on the wounds of Christ as pain we ourselves
inflicted upon him. Otherwise, mere relief from the guilt
of sin is sought, which is often only a temporary impulse.
The mercy of God is limitless, but this does not invite a
distortion of mercy's harder truth and the hard task of a
change of life after a conversion.*

Of its very nature, a conversion is an experience of
divine mercy. An exquisite gesture of divine regard
has taken place toward the uniqueness of our soul.
A lasting wisdom awaits us if we ponder deeply
the actual cost of divine mercy—the crucifixion
of Jesus of Nazareth for our own sins. The reception of God's forgiveness for sins, his mercy toward
our soul, implies always a remembrance of this cost.
Our own sins took him to the crucifixion. When
we lose sight of this connection, we falter in our
understanding of divine mercy, missing its enormous impact. According to Saint Thomas Aquinas,
mercy is the supreme attribute of God and, for that
reason, must be honored and loved in all its truth.
We have received it as a gift. But like any gift, it
ought not to be diminished in value because it has

been extended so freely to us. Rather, it should provoke a deepening humility in our lives. The prodigal son was certainly consumed with shame and regret when he made his decision to return to his father. The real test of his conversion, however, lay still in his future. His taste of mercy on his arrival home hopefully led to a prodigality of humble gratitude that never forgot the embrace of his father on that day. Humility of soul will always remain strong in a soul that understands the mystery of mercy.

~

Among the spiritual confusions of the current day, unfortunately, a misunderstanding of divine mercy is high on the list. For many people, God's mercy has shifted from divine forgiveness offered to the repentant sinner to a divine pity for the sinner who persists in sin and seems unable to extricate himself from his sin. In this understanding, mercy is directed primarily, not at the forgiveness of particular sins, but at the painful sense of *guilt* for sin. The sin itself is a secondary consideration, while mercy is somewhat like a spiritual blanket covering the soul with the warmth of divine compassion. Receiving mercy in this view does not at all require a struggle to overcome sin. Instead, it has become akin to an act of amnesty, a divine reprieve granted to the guilty conscience. It simply releases a soul from the burden of shame felt after committing sin. Such a notion strips personal conversion from the aim of God's mercy. No link exists between a sorrow for grave particular sins and a determination not to sin as a condition for receiving mercy. The sacrament of confession naturally fades in importance as the necessary means of returning to a state of grace when grave sins afflict a life. Instead, a soft, indulgent notion of God's love for sinners takes hold, that God is all merciful and non-judgmental in a general way, an avuncular figure instead of a true father, winking a blind eye at the misfortune of grave transgressions. Indeed, the virtual disappearance of the sense of sin, regardless of life-style and choices, will be for some souls the great manifestation of divine mercy. God's merciful acceptance, without a need for change, will monopolize a person's image of relations with God.

~

By divine power, God can perform an act of miraculous healing upon a bodily infirmity suffered by a man or woman. There is no requirement, spiritual or otherwise, for the recipient of such a miracle to exercise a prior faith in the possibility of the miracle. At times people are healed because others have prayed and interceded for them, unbeknownst to them. The one cured simply receives the extraordinary benefit of the divine act. But the mercy of God cannot be received in the same manner. It is received only by a person who allows the blood shed by Jesus on the Cross to be poured out upon his own soul. This is precisely what happens in every true conversion. Our Lord's suffering for our sins on the Cross is a mystery inseparable from the extension of mercy to our soul. This truth does not allow an indulgent understanding of mercy, as though we can receive mercy for our sins and then go on in life unfazed by the suffering of Jesus in his Passion. This forgetfulness of the Passion of Christ is surely the primary distortion in all false interpretations of mercy. The idea of mercy as an indulgent gesture toward the sinner does not just distort God's mercy. It violates a necessary awareness of the dreadful horror of a Roman crucifixion offered by Our Lord for our own sins. The idea of divine mercy becomes a bloodless notion without the sight of a man undergoing torture on a Roman cross in order to bring forgiveness of sin to repentant souls.

～

The truth of divine mercy is as such always linked to the sacrifice at Calvary. Mercy cannot be separated from the Passion of Christ if it is to remain in truth the mercy of God. Detached from the suffering of Christ at Golgotha, it becomes a fanciful

notion inviting false interpretations, and it does not
result in conversions. Rather than a cleansing of
the soul's sins through the blood of Christ, mercy
becomes palliative care of the sinner—a painkiller
applied to the misery of soul that ensues as a consequence of sin. Without our eyes on the agony
of the crucifixion, mercy is embraced greedily as
a panacea for the pains of conscience. We forget
that our own sins shred the body of Christ on the
Cross. Cut off from a remembrance of the torture
at Calvary, there is no reason for us to prostrate
ourselves in tears at the foot of the Cross, to feel
any disgust for serious sin, or even to seek repentance. This idea of mercy as a comforting salve for
sin, soothing our conscience of bereavement and
the pangs of regret, ultimately dismisses the aversion of God toward sin. The wound to the heart of
God caused by sin becomes of little or no concern.
The intense suffering of contempt and mockery in
Our Lord's Passion is ignored.

~

In chapter 22 of Saint Luke's Passion account, the
elegant robe that Herod took from his closet and
placed on the shoulders of Jesus on his last day
was a gesture of cold mockery. Tired, bored, con-
temptuous, Herod on an impulse gave away a rich
robe to the poor man of Nazareth and enjoyed the

mocking laughter that filled the room. Pilate and Herod became friends that day, we are told; before this they had been enemies. How so? Unlike Saint Luke, Saint Matthew in his Gospel writes of a scarlet robe wrapped around Jesus. If that detail is accurate, the sight of Our Lord returning to the praetorium, walking through an entryway into Pilate's presence, must have startled the governor's eye. The Roman officers wore red cloaks, and here, returning from Herod, was Jesus standing before him in a bright red garment like the pantomime of a Roman general returning from battle. It must have amused Pilate. He may have made a comment and drawn some laughter. And he would have a different appreciation for Herod after the gesture of giving away a rich robe for a moment of mirth. They became friends that day at the expense of the Lord's mockery, which is true of many friendships. As a result, despite his earlier sympathy, Pilate's respect for Jesus lessened, and he ordered his scourging, upon which he was brought before the crowd, brutally beaten and wearing a crown of thorns. In Saint John's Gospel, the red robe became purple after the scourging, no doubt from the blood soaking the cloth of that elegant robe. It was a robe wet with blood that Pilate may have seen in a last glance at Jesus' back before he walked away.

~

Is divine love actually *wounded* in heaven by a human betrayal? It is a question we cannot really answer. But it may be hard for us not to think that there must be a mystery of suffering in eternity when a soul once close to God forsakes him and turns down a destructive path. Doctrinally we uphold as Catholics that there is no suffering in the nature of God. But the love eternally present in Jesus' Passion at Calvary must have suffered the desertion of every soul who would reject him until the end of time. There may be a kind of divine perseverance in this painful awareness at Calvary that is one with the human heart of Jesus Christ on the Cross. The only analogy to it may be in the human heart that continues to love another person even after a betrayal. In Jesus' human heart, God must undergo some timeless mystery of loss even as he still pursues a soul destined to give itself away. Jesus suffered on the Cross in waiting for the end of his own Passion, and he suffered in knowing already the conclusive rejection that some souls would make toward him, allowing no reprieve. Every indication is that he is willing to suffer this terrible loss rather than overwhelm a soul with a grace that cannot be refused. The mercy of God cannot be understood in truth without this acknowledgment that souls do choose to reject his graces even to the end of their lives.

~

It is not only a bleak nihilism that strips meaning and the struggle for purpose from life. This can come also from a pseudo-religious attitude that adopts a view of God whose most certain feature is to ensure that in the end everyone is brought safely home to heaven. The assumption that after death heaven awaits all of us may in fact indicate how little actual thought has been given to a divine judgment upon our own life. It can be almost as though a soul thinks that it is making an offer God cannot refuse when it embraces an exaggerated confidence in divine mercy to protect itself from any possibility of a post-mortem tragedy. The mercy of God is limitless, and it is open to a soul to the last breath. But it must also be chosen by means of a cry for mercy coming from a heart repentant for sins.

~

Divine omnipotence is an attribute of God. Nonetheless we cannot say that we know God properly until we perceive his renouncement of an ultimate power over souls. This is not an act of sacrifice or abnegation on God's part, stripping himself of a possession he could use or that he formerly enjoyed. There exists rather a mystery in the exercise of divine power toward souls. God's love is infinitely powerful, and yet he does not exercise it simply as a power. His love is a communication to the one loved, inviting a response of love. Our

Lord will not overwhelm us and leave us without
an option of refusal. It seems no exercise of the
divine power of love ever leaves us incapable of a
refusal and an indifference to love. In this sense,
God makes himself powerless in love before our
choices. The vulnerability of God to the choice
of a human person is an amazing truth. It teaches
something proper in our own relations to others.
Any power over souls should be renounced with
an absolute determination, so that we do not ap-
propriate to ourselves a prerogative that God himself does not claim. Genuine love must be powerless in a certain sense before the one loved. This
condition for love identifies a clear truth of divine
love, not as a supplementary aspect of love, but in
its very nature. And so it must be true also of ourselves. The powerlessness of God in the merciful
love offered to souls provides a glimpse into the
abyss of divine love. But we need to reflect much
on this truth. Our effort to "win souls" to God
ought not to seek the satisfaction of a conquest and
personal triumph. Rather, we must participate in
the powerlessness of divine love before the freedom of a unique soul.

~

Compassion that seeks to ease the inner turmoil
and discomfort of those burdened by moral irre-
sponsibility is misplaced and false. Yet we see this

approach to souls much in the vanguard of pastoral ministry. There is often good reason for the inner oppression that afflicts souls immersed in serious sin. They are graced to undergo it; the pain they experience is a symptom of God in pursuit of them. The pain is part of the chase of divine mercy after souls. On the other hand, a benevolent sentimentality toward souls and their history of sin seems common today. Desiring to make people feel good about themselves, and no longer torn and conflicted, seems at times the only "holy" approach to souls. This disservice to souls ignores the true drama of interior struggle leading to conversions. It is a serious grace when a soul confronts the possibility of a tragic ruin of its life in its true magnitude; even more, when a soul faces God in truth and realizes the undetermined direction it might still take in life. Real compassion for another soul may be most poignant in fortifying someone with the strength to seek a great reversal of a life. God's mercy is concealed and yet immediate in these efforts on our part for others.

~

The divine knowledge of a soul is always a merciful knowledge. We can never be in a true relationship with God until we discover that we are *only* known mercifully. Not just loved with intermittent mercy after sinning and repenting once again, but that we cannot be looked at, that we cannot be known by God or drawn to him except as a soul in need, poor and destitute, incapable of avoiding collapse and ruin without divine intervention. A profound mercy, in other words, permeates God's vision of our soul. On our part, faithfulness to this mercy is to keep an awareness of the divine gaze upon our soul. It is to know ourselves as known by God in mercy. The soul conscious of mercy enters into prayer in poverty and need, but it also knows God's presence as a gaze of love upon its poverty. And its confidence in mercy becomes an implicit wonder and admiration directed toward God's attraction for the poverty at the heart of our soul.

~

The demonic presence is certainly real, even if many dismiss or ignore this reality. The mistake can be costly. For he always hides, all stealth and quiet steps and with what may seem an absence of passion for the soul being sought. This camouflage conceals at times an extreme patience, a sinister discipline the devil has acquired over time. It is a certain exercise of mastery over his impulsive pride. It is not inconceivable that a demonic presence may stalk a soul uneventfully through many years as though there were no end to merely observing it. But he watches the clock and marks the calendar. The waiting is never without plan and calculation. The demonic intelligence, in its pride, cannot conceive anything less than a victory. And sometimes this means ignoring many opportunities that might only lead to renewed tears and the repentance of a soul. Perhaps he saves his energy for a seductive attack at a late hour in life when a soul, after long years of respectable virtue and perhaps little love or concern for other souls, would find it insulting to acknowledge any personal contribution to Christ's crucifixion.

~

If we get closer to Third World poverty, even in our thoughts, and hold our gaze long enough, we cannot but ask certain questions. The terrible suffering of very poor people is unsettling. Not just the poverty of having little to spare, but real suffering that finds no alleviation, no rescue; suffering brutally endured. Diseased and victimized children, lives mutilated by anarchic violence, mothers torn apart in panic by their children's pain, grotesque cancers and deformed bodies, why such affliction? Does the divine plan include a place for such suffering? This mystery can be pondered only in reverent and silent incomprehension. And only one response is really possible. It must be that God in his mercy takes these lives into a hidden union with Jesus' own Passion on the Cross. Without their awareness, these suffering poor are sacrificial victims offered for others as part of a mercy of God for souls. Their lives, even as children, are united to the Cross at Calvary and bear their suffering in reparation for sins in the world. At first we may reject in that thought what seems to be an undeserved punishment inflicted on the innocent. It is the sinner who should suffer for his sin. But this objection misses the deeper truth of divine mercy. It is the choice of God to unite himself mysteriously to those who in any way share the Passion at Calvary. The poor in their own crucifixions may be entirely ignorant of this link. Yet Our Lord is not ignorant of them, and surely he knew them as he suffered his own agony on the Cross. And if we ask why such vast misery persists among the world's poor to our own day, perhaps the reason is because very few people offer sacrifice and prayer for souls in need of mercy; nor have there ever been more than a few. And so Our Lord turns to the poor.

~

Why were two men crucified on either side of Jesus at Calvary? An interior experience that the Virgin Mary underwent at Calvary is the possible reason. The account in Saint Luke's Gospel of the so-called good thief is well known. This man,

likely a murderer, rebukes the other crucified criminal for taunting Jesus and then turns to Jesus with
his request to join him when he comes into his
kingdom. This moment is the first deathbed conversion as Jesus extends the extraordinary promise
of mercy to him, that of being with him that day in
paradise. Surely Mary had prayed for his soul before his words to Jesus. He was at risk of losing his
soul, and he was saved in his last hour by embracing the offer of mercy. But what happened with the
"other" man at the crucifixion? The Gospel is quiet
and does not speak of any appeal to the mercy of
God. We have to assume that this man remained
full of venom and curses to the end. When the
soldiers broke the legs of these two criminals still
alive, they slowly suffocated on their crosses, unable to hold themselves up and breathe. Mary, in
terrible pain, stood watching their death agonies
as another soldier plunged his spear into the side
of Jesus, penetrating his heart. Yet the real pain of
this piercing took place in Mary, a dreadful suffering that she carried with her in memory even into
heaven. Despite her prayer and her desperate desire for the conversion of this other criminal, she
stood helpless before what was likely the death of
a man who refused any last act of repentance. In
that case, the piercing of the heart of Mary is inseparable from the death of the unrepentant criminal at Calvary. In some mysterious manner, it is an

experience she has never overcome, even now in heaven. Rather, it has carved into her immaculate soul an immense yearning to go in search for souls who are in danger of eternal loss. In a sense, all of history is at Calvary before the eyes of Mary as these two men die on either side of the cruci-fied Jesus. There are those who in sorrow for their sins embrace God's mercy, even on their deathbed; then there are those who refuse God and his mercy. Mary may have been given a deep intuitive vision of this division among souls at Calvary. Perhaps she has never forgotten that vision or the terrible pain it caused her to see a child of God lose his eternal soul; nor has she forgotten the tears she shed in that hour. It is why she begs us in her apparitions for prayer and sacrifice for the conversions of sinners.

~

The fact that few people give thought to the des-tiny of the "other criminal" at Calvary may indicate that we do not ponder seriously enough the possi-bility of the eternal loss of souls. The nebulous no-tion of a last-minute reprieve for all souls seems a better, more attractive option for one's hope. And, indeed, we must maintain committed hope for the salvation of even the most desperate sinner. But the horrific suffering of Christ may offer us a sober-ing reflection. The suffering at Calvary is immense because sins have been cruel and enormous in history. The redemptive act sealed in the suffering of the divine Son's flesh is in proportion to the sins of humanity throughout history. Another thought, however, should intrude. The suffering is so great because it is offered for the sake of the hardened sinner. The terrible agonies are Our Lord's last appeal to accept his mercy, especially for souls who have arrived at their own destitute conclusion of life, so emptied now after pursuing the seductions of evil. The death of Jesus is not just an execution. It is a brutal humiliation and degradation of a man. It is intended in the divine plan to conquer hearts that may have the grace to look toward a crucifix near the end of their lives. It is to provoke them to realize the cost of their own sins upon Our Lord. Any man, still in great sin and with death hovering nearby, who hangs from a cross of pain on some hospital bed can turn and realize mysteriously that this man who is God suffered for him. And certainly we can hope that the Virgin Mary is present then to help the cry for mercy pour out from his lips.

～

The reception of mercy, when it is dramatic and profound, will always urge us to seek the same gift for others. A missionary impulse enters into our soul in undergoing a conversion. We want the truth of God's mercy to be known, the taste of his presence to pierce others. We sense, not a burden here, but a desire animated by love. It is no different in one sense from a person suddenly in love. The world shines in a luminous appearance once the truth of a *personal* God and his mercy becomes undeniably evident to our soul. A definitive consent is made to God, a great "yes" to the privilege of his presence, and the desire is then strongly felt to spread the favor of his mercy that we have received. It is not surprising at all that great conversions among the saints—Saint Augustine, Saint Francis of Assisi, Saint Ignatius of Loyola, Saint Teresa of Avila, Blessed Charles de Foucauld—compelled these souls to a missionary bent of soul. They could not hoard their treasure in secrecy. They had to share what they found in God's mercy, even at much cost and frustration. It is a measure of the genuine depth of a conversion that a soul is driven to give witness now to its love for God. The truth encountered in the privacy of an hour with God becomes the truth proclaimed in a lifetime of witness to Christian faith.

5

A Transformed Love for Souls

All too late, experience has taught me that we should not evaluate people by their vices but, on the contrary, by what they have kept intact and pure, by what there is still left in them of childhood, however deep we have to search for it.

— Georges Bernanos

Never look down on a person unless you are picking him up.

— Mother Teresa

He placed before us the fact of sanctity. . . . He brought us to know the saints and mystics.

— Raïssa Maritain on Léon Bloy

A conversion is not just a change of life-style. The new recognition of God infuses strong desires in our soul that God should be known by others as we now know him. A kind of missionary zeal for souls can take hold of our heart and enter into our impulses with other people. We would like to see conversions spread contagiously among our contacts with people. More immediately we would be happy at times to bowl over an unbelieving soul with the overwhelming truth of God. This enthusiasm for winning souls may be naïve in its optimism regarding the appeal of God to people who do not know him. But, in another sense, it is sign of our love for God. And a zeal for souls as we continue life is essential to a love for souls. We taste a graced impulse in wanting to bring others to the truth of God and to Catholic faith. We have to be led by God in this love for souls, learning wisdom of heart and suffering for souls, if we truly want their conversion to the faith. Even God in his omnipotence cannot convert a soul that does not want to know him.

In a time of widespread indifference to faith, one dilemma in the effort to live for souls is whether to resist in a forceful manner a disdain for religious truth that we may encounter in others. It would seem that few victories take place. Even so, does the likelihood of rejection excuse us from a struggle that God may expect us to enter bravely, especially after our own conversion? Is it enough to comfort ourselves with the assurance that truth will win in the end? Perhaps a different recognition is possible. Truth was nailed to a Cross at Calvary in Jesus Christ. And it should be equally evident that the crucifixion of truth continues throughout the course of history. Should we expect otherwise in our own time? The ignominy and shame of Golgotha do not suggest great triumphs for those who defend and live Christian truths, including moral truths. The Cross implies, rather, that we will be crushed at times in an unequal fight. What God asks us to accept is that, if we are worthy of it, Christ will be mocked and scourged within our own life, even in trying to love and save souls. That mystery cannot take place unless we are courageous in our witness to Christian dogmatic and moral truth. We can trust that the experience of rejection is united to his mysterious presence and, perhaps, in the long run wins more souls than we can realize. Those with eyes to see will perceive this reality.

~

No one takes delight in mockery or rejection. Nor did Jesus Christ welcome them when he suffered the brutal rancor of the crowds during his Passion. But how else do we learn to love generously in some semblance of imitating Our Lord unless rejection is no longer experienced as a reproach to love itself? The soul that goes far in love after a conversion has learned to make no excuses in the realm of loving. It prefers to crawl in the dust in the effort to love and bring another soul to the truth rather than to surrender the determination to love. There is likely no saint ever who did not know firsthand the experience of a cutting disdain for his existence from some person in his life. The real lives of saints were often forged in the furnace of Golgotha's contempt.

~

"Trust witnesses who are willing to sacrifice their lives" (Pascal). It is a false notion that we can convince someone of a truth of faith simply by persuasive argument alone. Yet sometimes, after a conversion, we may think it is that easy. This is an excessive confidence in the power of reason. Believing is never the result simply of reasoning to a conclusion. Faith's initial flame catches fire when grace penetrates beyond merely rational understanding and provokes a deep attraction for the mystery of God. A choice to believe must occur. A soul must stand face to face before the *mystery* of Jesus Christ, because even in believing not all matters are comprehended. When a person receives the grace of faith and responds to it, another form of persuasion has ordinarily been at work. The entry into faith takes place most often by the impact of one soul upon another. An encounter with the heroic generosity and deep faith of a religious person is the most striking testimony to the truth of the Gospel. The spiritual vibrancy of persons who have intense faith, their generosity and full attention to the souls around them—these are more convincing arguments for the truth of Jesus Christ than any intelligent words) (Those who give up everything for God have always been the most powerful proof for the truth of Christ as a personal presence) But there is also a corollary to this. In a time when Christianity does not attract so strongly, must it be that souls giving their lives sacrificially to God are far fewer in number or perhaps simply more isolated, less visible, less able to influence? It is love alone in generous self-giving that consistently draws others to the truth of Jesus Christ.

~

The self-conscious rejection of any religious commitment can never be identical to what God sees in a soul. Nor should it be our view of a person who presently claims to have no faith. For it is God's way with every soul to seek and chase after it, never to accept a permanent estrangement. It is true that a soul can frustrate God's action and place barriers of stiff resistance to God's interventions, but no one has the power to terminate God's pursuit. All this occurs mysteriously, often at unseen layers of the soul. The desires of God for a soul remain hidden from sight. He may be drawing someone to himself long before that soul becomes aware of it. It reminds us perhaps that no one we encounter may be as resistant to faith as it appears initially.

At the very time when we might be dismayed by a person's absence of interest in God, even by an aggressive hostility toward religion, the mysterious attraction of God may already be rising up within that soul, perhaps soon to become known. And now and in days to come, God may want to use us precisely for such a person to be his sign of tender love for that soul. We cannot know God's hour of truth in such matters. His mercy may be much closer than we think.

~

Our Lord's words to his apostles at the Last Supper—"Apart from me you can do nothing" (Jn 15:5)—do they imply that with him we can accomplish all things as long as we ask God to accompany our effort to lead others to him? In the long term, we must surely trust in this divine promise and assurance. Yet, in the current hour, the possibility of failing is always quite real whenever we attempt to bring people closer to Christ. But does defeat at the moment mean that God's desire has been thwarted? What seems a failure to win a soul to Christ may hide grace beneath the rubble of our toil and heartache. Our ineffective efforts may have left behind a concealed influence, but perhaps only if we have exposed our conviction about God quite nakedly and have allowed our spiritual poverty to be plainly seen. We may experience this poverty when we find ourselves facing an utter disinterest toward what we most revere and love. Perhaps it can be like a woman who sees the husband she loves dishonored and disrespected in her presence. Yet in God's mysterious ways of grace, the poverty we may experience then may not be fruitless in its hidden influence on another soul.

~

An impassioned response leaping into action contrasts certainly with a detached emotional reaction. But what do these differences say about our soul? Not perhaps what we think. It is not always the case that outward restraint in manner is a sign of deeper spiritual quality. Far better sometimes, for the sake of loving souls and seeking their salvation, to be seized and tossed about by passion than to esteem too highly the preservation at all cost of our own composure. A perpetual calm may be conserved at times only by giving greater importance to self than to the demands and disorders of life calling for some personal response of love to win others to Christ. The upheavals and turmoil we face are often of grave import in matters of truth and call for our entry into the fray when souls are at stake. Unfortunately, we may come home dirtied and torn and even bloodstained. And yet if God is pleased with our effort to love souls and give witness to faith, this is all that matters. After a struggle with indifference to God, we may face a harder hour of prayer than a steady calm might provide. But God surely has his way to compensate for this.

~

"Truth is a power, but only when one does not demand that it have immediate effect" (Romano Guardini). To approach someone in any spiritual danger without probing unnecessarily or trying to satisfy a curiosity, moved simply by a desire for the spiritual welfare of another, means to limit ourselves initially to knocking on a door and waiting for an invitation to enter. Unfortunately, the door may remain shut and no entry granted. Even in the zeal to save another from harm, the door ought not to be broken down, lest an escape out the back window take place and a disappearance from our lives forever. Souls at risk often need our abiding for a time in prayer for them and a willingness to befriend them gradually rather than to stage a dramatic rescue.

~

A tendency to willfulness may test every soul that aspires to love the souls of others and bring them to the knowledge of Christ and the Church. Under the cover of zeal and good intentions, much of what we do may conceal self-interest. This willfulness is hard to detect because the pride behind it is easily unnoticed. When pride drives our activity, even to do good for others and to lead them to truth, everything done is impure to some degree. We force our way through doors instead of gently knocking. We push our plans and want quick results and accomplishments for the good of others. We forget God's timing and the need to wait upon his hidden work. The self-willed person may seem often to achieve results in a certain manner. But if we look more closely, we will see that what we do with an aggressive zeal has a superficial spiritual quality. These efforts do not draw people so much to God, and for good reason. What they really seek may be the submission of another's will to our own will. Much harm can sometimes be done in the spiritual realm of affecting souls without patience to let God be God. He will show himself and his desire to others in due time the more we are self-effacing and allow him to act secretly. Often this divine action is gradual and takes time.

~

The increase of spiritual awareness after a conversion produces a different quality of eye. With greater love, we see the faces of other people with more penetration and insight. What explains this? For one thing, love draws our soul toward what is real simply for the sake of knowing it. Our eyes become more disinterested in their attention. They take in more, with no grasping for knowledge in an acquisitive way. We receive the person before us with greater openness to sheer presence alone, not to evaluate or compete or reduce to some category. Moreover, the receptivity given in love draws us toward what is unseen, a deeper truth in another, the need for God. This concealed realm of need in another person is often a secret of suffering, a hidden poverty that has entered a life to the degree that the human hunger to be loved has been frustrated. Love allows this poverty, often buried under the scarred coarseness of an external personality, to rise up and make contact with our eyes. The more we see this poverty of a soul needing God, the more we may find a desire erupting in us that souls come to know Jesus Christ.

~

The story of Zacchaeus in chapter 19 of Saint Luke's Gospel, the man who climbed a sycamore tree in Jericho for a better view of Jesus coming down the path, raises a question. How did Jesus know his name? While the first thought may be by divine knowledge, the answer can be more human in context. This man Zacchaeus, short of stature and despised as a tax collector, a functionary of the Roman occupation, has probably climbed his tree awkwardly. The impression upon the imagination does not suggest an athletic man. Perhaps he managed to tear a bit of his more stylish clothes on the way up. As Jesus draws near, it is likely that the crowd has already been tormenting Zacchaeus at the spectacle of this little man clinging tightly to a branch to keep from falling. The sight invites mockery and jeers from the crowd, and they probably shout Zacchaeus' name with insults and disparagement. When Jesus looks up to address him, then, he is quite aware of his name. And he is not just kind in calling to him, but he addresses him *with respect*, in contradiction to the humiliating banter that surrounds Zacchaeus. "Make haste and come down; for I must stay at your house today" (Lk 19:5). One cannot help but think that a smile is on the lips and in the heart of Jesus in speaking these words. Zacchaeus, perhaps a bit portly, will have a hard time hurrying down a tree before welcoming Jesus to his home for dinner. And of course the smile is even greater as Jesus observes this man's heart open to him in conversion, his only friend at that hour.

～

When we do not really love, is it because our relations with people have become something of an
exercise in abstract thought? Is this not what every
form of shallow judgment is—to analyze, classify,
categorize persons, to arrive at rapid conclusions after contact with external features? Perhaps one way
to counter this tendency is to recall that the knowledge of a person that comes with genuine love is
never a knowledge that acquires advantage over another. It never reduces or immobilizes another person; it is never a power of any sort. The knowledge given in love is not a conclusion, but a new
beginning sought over and over again. It compels
us always to pass beyond our previous experience
to a fresh vision of another person. Conversions
demand a transformation in our habits of looking
at people. When we begin to perceive more often
the presence of an eternal soul in people, a sense
of sacredness affects our encounters. Then, more
often, we will exercise a quiet, stronger influence
upon souls.

~

We would be better off at times with defective
memories. Perhaps we should pray for this. A loss
of memory would allow us to see other people
without at times the sharp-edged remembrance of
previous encounters with them. It can be a valuable
spiritual discipline to look at a person with fresh

eyes and a pure, untainted perception, as though for the first time. It is an effort that can be surprising in its discoveries. We might find more often a quiet loneliness existing in a person we thought we knew, missed until then when all along it was hiding in a face. We have only to open our eyes more to perceive this truth, without a background of burdensome memory to encumber them. Many souls suffer their lack of God, and we need to sense in some way this deeper spiritual loneliness. The sight of a deeper poverty in another soul not only draws our compassion. Often a soul without God recognizes in some way that it is known at last, with a different understanding from another. It is a first step, perhaps, to realizing God's gaze of mercy inviting that soul to return home.

～

The saints in certain cases were said to enjoy the charism of a special knowledge of souls. Sometimes this referred to knowledge of the sins that burdened another soul, other times to accurate intuitions about God's will for a life. It should not be surprising that saints had this gift. They entered into truth wherever it was to be found, including the inner truth of souls. If they had a deeper knowledge of souls, it was because God's love for these souls was present within their own hearts. There can be a caricature of this type of spiritual insight, however, when we are not saints ourselves. It involves the pretension of piercing through the mask of appearance to the inner truth of another, squeezing and kneading it in our grip, identifying the hidden reasons behind defect and deficiency. We have to relinquish psychological habits of this sort as a form of disrespect toward souls. But this is only possible when we keep in mind that the soul of the other is a secret that remains beyond our limited sight, known fully to God alone. Any glimpse of truth that the saints had into souls through love was not simply a form of knowledge. It was ignorance as well, a holy unknowing, an ultimate incomprehension of love's power to find beauty when at first the soul in front of us offers no initial attraction.

~

The effort to love someone difficult to love usually means receiving no return for love when we make an effort of love. But should we expect a different striving, as though victories were the only worthwhile pursuit? If, after an arduous effort to love another, we are still committed in the desire to love, or at least humbled in our effort to love, it is for the moment enough. The aspiration to love remains alive in every attempt at love. It may be all God desires from us at times, the willingness to persevere in the effort even when failing. But these efforts must be real words, real kindness, real patience and silence, real gestures of concrete aid —and always with the thought that a *soul* is present before our eyes, and its salvation may be at stake. Our own conversion should remind us that we, too, may have been very difficult to love before God showed his kindness to us.

~

The content of a conversation is not so important sometimes if we want to love another person and lead him to Christ. What is important is the capacity to perceive the presence of a hidden poverty in another person. At times this poverty, this lack of belief, is revealed, not exactly by what is said, but in a tone of voice, in its repetitions, in its silences, or perhaps by an inability to arrive at any expression of personal conviction. All this must enter a silence within our own soul if we are to find in another's poverty of unbelief an attraction drawing our love. And yet this sight of poverty in another is not a hard discovery after a while. It is present all around us these days. Once we have seen it and experienced love for another as a result, it tends to return to our perception.

~

Conversions always infuse a quiet urgency into the life of charity. Once a certain threshold is passed in the recovery of grace, the spiritual life demands quick, alert responses, no delay or hesitation, but rather movement in haste—like the Virgin Mary's quick departure to visit Elizabeth in her need. The demands of love often cannot wait for deliberation before they are answered. There can be a sense of immediacy in love's awareness, and it is due to love's urgency. To delay and lose time when love can be exercised right now for a soul in need is to throw away an irrecoverable chance. And every opportunity weighs significantly after a time. A slow response, or, worse, a refusal, can afflict us later. Rather, we must respond as though a whole life concentrated its magnitude and density right in the present moment. Little preparation is even desirable to face the request of God in the present moment. We often need simply good eyes sensitive to a need for attention in a poor soul. The test is to realize that nothing more important matters than the person in front of us in that instant. And, indeed, no greater truth does matter than an encounter with a divine request to give our whole-hearted love in that hour. Who knows but that the salvation of a soul is at stake even in our initial contact with a person.

∼

The presence of love in the saints must have had a concealed dimension always. Goodness was seen in their actions, but perhaps rarely was the greater mystery of their love perceived. The internal impetus in it contained a deeper desire than their visible endeavors showed and always stretched beyond concrete actions. No doubt they always had an implicit desire that other souls should come to know God and know that they were loved by God. This desire surely surpassed any pragmatic consideration in actions. Indeed, they perhaps never sought merely practical consequences in actions. Nonetheless, the effect of their love could not always have been so evident for the ones they loved. And sometimes it may have been to a great extent never understood, at least in the present moment. Yet God was present whenever a saint was present, leaving some trace of his love for a soul.

∼

It is one of the more quiet truths of Catholicism that souls at times freely surrender long-guarded secrets as though this self-revelation is the most natural conversation that can take place. The visiting rooms of cloisters and monasteries have always known this, and priests of course know it in confessionals—people never seen before coming to unburden their darkest truths at a first encounter.

Perhaps it happens because God's eyes are strangely felt in the presence of a monk or priest or nun, and this releases the floodgates of dark reminiscence with no thought of caution, only a desire for purging. Indeed, it may be that the first hour of many conversions, sometimes near the end of lives, coincides with this sense of being already well known upon entering into the presence of a man or woman whom God is mysteriously using to disguise his own openhearted embrace.

~

After our own experience of conversion, we should trust that there is a kind of vulnerability for God in everyone, a spark in the soul ready to flame up toward God at unexpected moments. Often it takes misfortune, a tragedy, a personal loss, and then the vigilance against God suddenly gives way. The crushing moment has become a divine knock at the soul's door. The suffering has become a merciful gesture. We cannot know this by looking from the outside, but we should always respect its possibility. A personal misfortune may mean salvation for a soul, and we should take care to tread gently, not to get in God's way, and yet to be ready to be his instrument.

6

Seeking the Will of God

What do my tastes matter, O Lord; for me there is nothing more than thyself.

—Saint Teresa of Avila

Why are we going to want it, if God does not want it?

—Saint Maria de las Maravillas

You know what to do with your farm, and does God not know what to do with you, his servant?

—Saint Augustine

A conversion is the beginning of a lifelong engagement with the will of God. The saints tell us that a complete union of our will with the will of God is the ultimate goal of life, inseparable from our love for God. This surrender of ourselves to God faces test after test in life. Knowing God's will with some sense of certainty is the initial dilemma. Yet we may discover that this difficulty is matched at times by the ease with which God in his providence makes his desires known in the depth of our heart. He is always leading us to truth if we are ready to recognize it. Choosing is still another thing. Relinquishing our own desires and preferences once we know what God wants and giving ourselves to God's choice is a conversion we must seek many times in life. We experience this demand strongly at the outset of a conversion. It is an early taste of a need repeated throughout life to seek his light patiently, waiting upon his direction and his lead. God's interest in our regard is always to bring us into some deeper conformity with his own will.

"Do you love me more than these?" (Jn 21:15). The resurrected Christ asked this question of Saint Peter, on the shore of the Sea of Galilee, in the glow of an early morning sunrise. It is often thought a question whether Peter's love for Jesus is greater than the love the other disciples have for him. The word "these" would refer to the others present, as though a competition is taking place and Peter must renew his determination to win. But surely this is an incorrect reading. Jesus will not ask us whether we love him more than another person loves him. He *will* ask whether we intend to love him entirely to our last drop of blood—not a small thing. Then to what is Jesus referring by the word "these"? After Our Lord called from the shore to cast a net to the side of the boat, the great catch of 153 fish occurred. Naturally it stirred immense excitement. Jesus himself was waiting on the shore as they pulled this load in. But who counted the fish?

A reasonable guess would be Peter, who had already shown an impulsive excitability—at the Transfiguration, for instance, and in the arrest of Jesus in Gethsemane. The Gospel implies that Jesus' question of love was spoken privately to Peter as they began a walk along the beach with the sun rising to the east. Perhaps Our Lord pointed at the pile of fish and gestured to the shimmering water in the rising sun when he pronounced the words "do you love me more than *these*?" Do you love your fish, Peter, and the beauty of the sunrise on the sea more than me? Would you return to this life and choose this peace and repose over me? The question echoes into the heart of every soul yearning for God after a conversion. Would we choose anything or anyone over him?

～

The encounter with the resurrected Christ at this site on the Sea of Galilee offers another lesson. Our Lord's manner of instruction is not always in words, but it is nonetheless clear. The command to cast the net to the side of the boat repeats a request Jesus made to Saint Peter three years earlier on the day he called Peter and Andrew, James and John, to follow him. The account described in Saint Luke's fifth chapter recalls as well that Peter is first told to put out to deeper water, to which

Peter protests in a weary tone that he has fished all night long, catching nothing. But he will do so, he says, at the Lord's command. The description in the Gospel suggests that only half the instruction is observed. The boat is perhaps never taken out to deeper water. The nets are simply dropped, not so far from shore. Yet the miracle takes place, an enormous catch of fish filling the nets. "Depart from me", says Peter, in fear, "for I am a sinful man" (Lk 5:8). "Do not be afraid;" Jesus replies, "henceforth you will be catching men" (Lk 5:10). Three years later, the parallel event at the Sea of Galilee is a sharp, piercing reminder to Peter of Jesus' words at the earlier miracle to be fearless. For now the time has come to give all his energy and zeal to catching men. No more fishing on a peaceful lake; those days are over. And so when Jesus questioned Peter—"Do you love me more than these?" (Jn 21:15)—it was to draw from him as well a resolute determination to live henceforth for the salvation of souls. And it is precisely this determination to live *for souls* that marks a man or woman who has crossed a threshold of deeper insight into the real meaning of conversion.

~

There must occur a deeper recognition in prayer after a serious conversion that we are called to a *mission*, a sacred purpose that at first is not specified in any concreteness but that unfolds with time. For most people, the recognition may not come until after they have embraced their vocation to married or religious life or the priesthood. At some point, there is a deeper sense given of an expectation that God personally addresses to our soul. He desires the pursuit of a task within a vocation. It is nothing less than the mysterious voice of Our Lord that communicates this sense of a special task in our life. He may not speak in words, but we seem still to know. The message is uncompromising and clear. The initial revelation of it may be quiet, barely a whisper in the depths of the heart. Yet whispers, too, when they come from God, can be unmistakable in their direct, immediate command. This communication is a discovery within the soul that a unique fruitfulness awaits our soul if only we cleave now to this promise and light.

∼

The discomfort in youth of not knowing what God wants from our life has dangers. There is always the possibility of impulsive decisions and false steps, sometimes precipitated by the need to overcome the anxiety of an ongoing state of irresolution. But the more regrettable mistake occurs when there *is* an invitation from God, and no choice is made. Often it may be that a young soul after a conversion does not embrace this grace of invitation because it cannot bear the uncertainty that accompanies a special call from God. It does not accept that the uncertainty of not knowing clearly what God wants must be passed through. It is an early test of faith. A young man or woman may assume that it is customary for God to manifest his will with some sign of radiant clarity. Lacking that sign, it seems there must be no special call. But God does not ordinarily provide this favor. Never finding himself under a flash of blinding light, a young person adopts an attitude of waiting for the definitive sign. In this manner, some people perhaps live a good portion of their youth brushing against the edge of the deeper offering they are meant to embrace, but never crossing a threshold of decision. They are stirred with desire, but they never risk a choice, and this malaise of indecisiveness gets into the fiber of their soul. A kind of hesitation enters into them, a state of perpetual indetermination that ends up defining their character, affecting their religious commitment for the rest of their lives. They do not realize that the genuine sign they were receiving of God's call to them was in the desire that was drawing them to God. The desire to give all of oneself to God, when it is present, is itself precisely the confirmation of the need to go forward.

~

To remain uncertain for a time after a conversion about what God wants from us, unsure of his desire, may be spiritually preferable, despite the lack of peace it brings, to an easy confidence that all is well and no questions need be asked. It takes courage to consider that the path on which we seem securely placed is not necessarily the choice God would make for us if he were consulted. Many times we may find that praying in a more direct and personal way the inimitable words of Jesus— "not my will, but yours, be done" (Lk 22:42)—is followed soon by an intervention in our life that shakes our complacency. Forsaking in prayer our own will, choosing intensely to surrender to his will, is never an act without consequence. What follows in life is never by chance or coincidental. The prayer in effect invites God to draw close, to come near, to reassert his unmistakable presence. We should not be surprised that he then does so. Yet he reveals himself invariably in disguise, always leaving us capable of missing his quiet word if we are not ready and longing for it.

~

The most common patterns for this disguise of communication after a conversion involve God using an improbable, unsuitable person to speak his desire to us and rouse some form of offering from our soul. Sometimes a person with no obvious place in our life to offer advice confronts us unexpectedly with a spiritual challenge, a challenge that has been brooding already in our soul, suppressed and neglected, until now with these words it cannot be ignored. Another time someone brings a steady trial into our life that does not disappear but, rather, becomes a daily dreaded presence in our life, and again God is speaking his will to us, asking for the sacrifice of humble patience from us. Other times the ambassador of God hides behind the tattered ruins of a poor soul, offering to us an insight of new respect for human suffering because we allow ourselves a conversation with a poor man. In all this we might remember that a refusal to accept that God speaks through unlikely instruments shows a serious lack of faith. Knowing God's will is not meant to be a remote and inscrutable task. On the contrary, his will may be ready to speak to us very nearby, as close to us as the next stranger's glance in our direction.

~

When does confidence in God speaking directly to our soul cross the line into presumption? It is a hard question to answer after a conversion inasmuch as souls can be led in ways that contradict common and ordinary paths. The soul that is absolutely sure of God's guidance and decides in accord with an inner light it is convinced comes from God has to be respected. Time will tell after a conversion whether the voice of God was actually speaking. And yet even if God has communicated, all is not finished. On the contrary, answering a command from God after the experience of conversion is only a beginning. The initial "yes" is decisive, but there is also the ongoing test of constancy. One thing does seem invariably true. Once a soul responds to God's call and instruction, the voice of God descends into a silence and a place of mystery within the soul. This means that we have to seek God continually in prayer in order to avoid mishap and detour. On the other hand, any claim of absolute clarity about what God wants, implying a clear picture of the future, may be a sign of some spiritual naïveté. It is much more likely that God grants to our soul only the yearning to plunge ahead, in surrender to him, without all directions in place. The days to come will provide later confirmation and further discovery. God prefers, it seems, that we allow him to lead us one step at a time, blindly clinging to the whisper of his voice. We are given no spiritual map in hand, outlined in red, for our life's spiritual journey. We have to cling to a hand that leads us only one short day at a time.

~

Is there something more to give God that until now has been withheld? Something essential that calls for recognition? Something I am refusing to see? The question of a possible blindness in our soul can have a way of rising up at times in the silence of prayer without a satisfactory answer. Other times the questions take on a different look, shifting to the past, causing another kind of disturbance. Was a request from God missed? An invitation ignored? A road not taken? The temptation in that case is to search for reasons that might explain the mistaken turns of our life. In both sets of questions, the answer to a riddle is sought, with the idea that some correction is possible. A failure or an oversight might be reversed, an omission recognized. Yet God may not be asking from us any such discovery or amendment. What he may desire at present is simply our complete surrender to his will in our current circumstances. That is enough, and yet it is also a very difficult thing. This must be a surrender that cuts deeply and irrevocably into our soul, and it is not easy. It is another form of conversion. But if it does take place, this quality of a deep surrender to God can remain a permanent disposition in our life of prayer. The need for such surrender may be the primary reason why such questions at times disturb us in prayer. God allows them after an initial conversion so that we accept all the foibles and misdirection of our life and then offer ourselves once again to him in a complete manner.

∽

Some years ago the Metropolitan Museum of Art in New York City held a special exhibition in which all the paintings in the exhibit shared Franciscan themes and inspiration. Father Benedict Groeschel, founder of the C.F.R. community of Franciscans, made a request to the museum to permit his brothers and priests to enter the museum an hour before the usual opening time so that they could meditatively enjoy these paintings without the press of the crowds. The community received the permission. At the end of their visit, as the men in their grey Franciscan robes were leaving the building, a line waiting for the museum to open had formed outside the building. An older woman caught the eye of one friar and called to him. "Sir, please, can you tell me, are you *for real*, or are you part of the exhibition?" The friar answered "Yes, we are for real." But the question did not disappear so quickly. He recounted that for a full week that same question kept interrupting his prayer—"are you *for real*?"—starkly reminding him how easy it is to be part of an external show without giving much and how deeply committed in love we must be to seek with passion a life with God.

~

God has eyes already for the future and knows what he wants to grant each life after a conversion. But this will mean that nothing is ever conclusive in his giving to us, nothing final and complete, until we have finished our days. And it may be that God, with his eyes already on what he intends to accomplish in love for our soul and the use he wants to make of us, will seem to reverse the course and direction that he had earlier set our soul upon. We cannot really prepare for such surprises. But we can know in faith that the whole of a life is contained within a single gaze of God. And although that gaze is imponderable and likely to make us anxious at times, it is wise to remember often the kindness of those eyes.

~

Deeper union with God after a conversion is due always in one sense to a fixed and stubborn adherence to the divine will. For that reason alone, the souls closest to God are going to appear at times incapable of flexibility and compromise. Negotiating with them on matters of importance to them is not generally auspicious for the contrary point of view. But these are not souls interested simply in winning arguments or getting their way. There is a fire in them for truth and for God that inflames them beyond their own human character whenever a question of truth or of God's will is at stake. The mere occasion of some challenge to their understanding of God's will is sufficient at times to arouse their mettle. To the outsider, it may seem that an arbitrary attachment is at work. But this is not often correct. It is the nature of a love for God in these souls that they rise up in vigor when confronted with opposition to what they sense is God's desire. They can be like a large wave unleashed from unseen depths of water in their refusal to halt once they have identified God's desire. Mother Teresa was certainly of this quality. Any priest, for example, who challenged her congregation's practice of frequent transfers of sisters was quickly informed of God's preference to use the poorest instruments to accomplish his most important works.

~

At certain times there is no proper interior choice but a blind confidence that God has intervened with his own choice when a sudden change is imposed on us. This can occur, for example, in unexpected serious illness or for religious or priests in the transfers they must accept. When there is no preparation and the change is sudden, there may seem no continuity or pattern to give meaning to abrupt transitions of this sort. The logic that ought to link one period of life to another is lacking. Do we expect, then, that God should explain himself? No, it is surely better that we not seek to remove our incomprehension about why God has chosen as he has. It may be his intention that we do not understand, just as we do not grasp his mystery in other efforts of searching. He conceals himself in these changes just as he does in prayer, no doubt so that we should entrust our soul blindly and unreservedly to him. The blind entrustment of our life to the unseen purposes of God is a form of spiritual conversion that is essential many times in life. And it will be necessary if at any time misfortune strikes us.

~

The sacred words "thy will be done" cannot be prayed except in realizing that much in our lives still awaits discovery. The words are a request for this truth to reveal itself. The genuine value of making this appeal to God depends on accepting already what God plans for us, even as it is unknown to us. The surrender to God of what we cannot yet know in his plan is a measure of our love for God.

The prayer is an act of confident anticipation that must be made without fear or hesitation, even if it will mean some taste of suffering in our lives. It is true that Jesus trembled and sweat blood in pronouncing these words "thy will be done" in Gethsemane, knowing the profound suffering that would intensify in a short time. We, however, must embrace these words, not with foreboding, but as a means of immediate entry into the heart of God. The conversion we need sometimes is largely in overcoming our anxiety and fear. Once we have crossed a threshold into his heart, we can trust, even in the likelihood of some future suffering, that in every circumstance we will have no desire to depart from him.

~

A subtle, almost paradoxical, obstacle in giving our will fully to God can be willfulness in the act. Fervent souls who are intense in their desire for God may take the lead too much in their relations with God. Their own will and self-interest direct their lives under the guise of pursuing goodness and virtue. In their eagerness sometimes to do great things for the love of God, an undercurrent of egotism may be somewhat present. They would do better to quiet down their zeal a bit and become more receptive to God. Perhaps this is unavoidable in most conscientious spiritual lives. Nonetheless, if not corrected, the result will be a life of visible good works, an admirable accomplishment to some degree, but in truth it may be more façade than solid structure with a crumbling foundation of vain motivations beneath it. A conversion by which our motives are purified is sometimes needed.

∼

One trait of false humility is that it inclines us to fatalism about circumstances and events without admitting the lack of courage in this attitude. It conceives humility as docility to God's control over our destiny, requiring only our non-interference. It accepts passively that all matters can be left to God and divine providence. But we should not call this humility. It may be a way simply to limit frustration at God's actual choices, an unwillingness to invest ourselves in ways that may lead at times to disappointment. The desire to find what pleases God has an uncertain quality in its demand. The failures that regularly ensue in the effort to know God's will teach actual humility, which always makes us more dependent on God. Conversely, the reluctance to risk mistakes in the search for God is a way to cut losses at the outset. But it will bring neither true humility nor any real offering of our life to God.

∼

"Ask, and it will be given you; seek, and you will find; knock, and it will be opened to you" (Lk 11:9). The words of Jesus identify a necessary disposition in prayer, though not, perhaps, only in their usual meaning. These words invite us to make confident requests to God, expecting that he will respond, at least in some manner. But the same words or a variation of them can become our own words to God. "Ask, Lord, and you will receive from me; seek, Lord, you will find what you look for; knock, Lord, and I shall open to you." Instead of making a request to God, we can invite his request to us. Perhaps it is a crucial spiritual act, for it may well be that God does not draw so near to our soul unless we solicit his unknown desire and accede to him in anticipation the surrender to all he will ask. "Give God permission" was a favorite refrain of Mother Teresa. It is a very deliberate choice, surely, to make ourselves more accessible to God and his will, leaving a door in our soul permanently ajar for him to do as he pleases.

～

We might ask whether there were impulsive, random acts by Jesus, acts without purpose. Healing one person, but not another? A turn down one road rather than another? Cursing this fig tree and not that one? Did every event involving Our Lord have some design and ultimate reason? If we answer yes, as no doubt we should, we are acknowledging as well that even the smallest hours in our lives can be part of the divine plan for our souls. On the other hand, to discern God's desires in the smaller choices of life can seem impossible. And yet this knowledge must be sought after a conversion if we are to enjoy closer, more contemplative relations with a God transcendent in mystery but near in his concealment. It is easy enough to expect that decisions of serious consequence in our lives will be guided by God. When we are facing important choices, God has his own way of making his preference known. But a God who descended to a crib and the obscurity of a carpenter's shop may want alertness to his presence even in the smallest choices. He wants all in a life to be offered to him. If we do not attend to that thought daily, we miss many opportunities for an offering to him that otherwise could be thought simply the endurance of a day's difficulties.

~

It may be that an unacknowledged desire to be left alone by God sometimes weighs in upon our private religious convictions about his relations with us. There can be a kind of laziness in our thoughts about God that we refuse to examine or question. These thoughts are damaging to the degree they are contrary to truth, and they require conversion.

An implicit conviction, for instance, of God's un-concern for our manner of living as long as no grave sin is committed is a distortion of God, placing him at a false distance from us. Such thinking must be confronted, or we will live without a personal God. If we have pushed God away to a peripheral side interest, it will surely take a disciplined effort to become unguarded again and realize that God is closer and more personal than our thought allowed. And certainly that kind of conversion is essential for most people at some time in life even after they have returned to the life of grace. But it is essential for another reason. Those not alert to God's actual proximity and presence in common daily events will not recognize as blessings the shocking interventions that God may later offer a life when he brings more formidable tests of his love.

~

Finding and embracing God's will can seem akin to a discovery we repeat over and over again in life, and, indeed, every day. Our thought can be that the more accurately and efficiently we identify the concrete choices that are the divine will for our life, the more God rewards our soul. But is this an accurate description of what union with God's will is? Does it not, for one thing, leave out the dilemma of a difficulty and darkness in knowing

God's will? Is there not an additional need to desire God even without a clear light to know what
he wants from us? Indeed, it may well be that the
desire for God in itself draws us to God's will even
without choices. This may be especially so when
we are unsure what God is asking of us. A desire to please God can be aflame in us quite in-
dependently of any decision or particular choice.
This wanting of God and longing for him already
unites us to God. The desire in itself becomes a
way of becoming conformed to God's will prior
to any choice. It is in itself a manner of finding
him and remaining ready for all that he will ask
of us. And it is a preliminary disposition necessary
for knowing what God wants when he chooses to
reveal his will.

~

What can we know with any certainty about God's
will for our daily life? Perhaps we can know very
little if we expect to identify particular actions as
God's direct request for us to choose. But even
with uncertainty, we can yearn for him, and this
in itself ensures that we will receive guidance that
we cannot possess of ourselves. Indeed, this desire
will often mysteriously place us where God wants
us in the current hour. The experience of being
where God desires in our encounters with people

is a repeated phenomenon in any life seeking him. It is as much an irrefutable element of genuine religious experience as more extraordinary manifestations of God's interventions in a human life. It is a fruit of all genuine experiences of conversion.

7

A New Vision of the Poor

What does love look like? It has the hands to help others. It has the feet to hasten to the poor and needy. It has eyes to see misery and want. It has the ears to hear the sighs and sorrows of men. That is what love looks like.

—Saint Augustine

All the destitute look to our hands just as we look to those of God when we are in need.

—Saint Basil

Nothing so much wins love as the knowledge that one's lover desires most of all to be himself loved.

—Saint John Chrysostom

The poor hide the presence of Jesus Christ beneath their exterior appearance. It is a secret that is sometimes revealed soon after a conversion. The roughness at the surface of poor lives is a disguise for the sacred presence of Our Lord himself. When a serious conversion takes place, the hunger for God that now animates the soul makes it desire contact with his presence. It will go in search to find him in his hiding places. Often, by God's favor and grace, a love for the poor suddenly awakens in the heart to meet that need. Perhaps it is God's way of confirming the genuine depth of a conversion. This love for the poor does not just urge us to practice charity to the poor. The concealed presence of Our Lord is drawing us toward the poor just as the Eucharist draws us to prayer. He is offering his friendship in the mysterious way of veiled encounters with his real presence. The consequence can be a lifelong need to keep the poor close to our lives.

The mysterious effect of a conversion is often felt in a changed experience of the poor. Suddenly we become sensitive to their presence when previously they may have been ignored. It is as though an invisible guide at our side is pointing in their direction, identifying them, and they have become more noticeable in the streets. The new awareness should not be surprising. Our Lord is now seeking our soul in a deeper way, offering us opportunities for an encounter with himself beyond prayer alone. He seems to awaken sympathy in our heart for the poor, which can quickly become a desire to engage poor persons in concrete ways. Once we cross that threshold, we may find that Our Lord uses these encounters to speak at times in mysterious half-whispers to us. The poor may acquire a sacred and special place in our heart, as though a gift has been given to us which must now be treasured. At the very least, the poor become a chance to express our gratitude to God after a conversion. And more and more we perceive a reality that earlier may have remained completely outside our view.

~

A serious conversion should always have this effect of altering our vision of the poor. Once we have discovered Christ in a personal encounter, the new awareness should rouse our desire for his hidden presence wherever he may be found. So often after a conversion, the Eucharist draws a soul strongly toward the intimacy of receiving him in Holy Communion or simply to be in his silent presence before a tabernacle in a church. But before long, an insight and recognition can awaken once we ponder the twenty-fifth chapter of Saint Matthew's Gospel. "I was hungry and you gave me food, I was thirsty and you gave me drink, I was a stranger and you welcomed me, I was naked and you clothed me. . . . Truly, I say to you, as you did it to one of the least of these my brethren, you did it to me" (Mt 25:35–40). The stark appeal in this declaration heard soon after a conversion takes many souls captive. We are ready then to hear the undiluted impact of these words and understand them literally. And surely this is how

Our Lord wants them to be heard. He has identified himself with the poor so that we can meet his
real presence in the poor. The converted soul hungry for him may easily find this truth a stunning
revelation. Our Lord is never far away. The closest
poor person offers an immediate contact with his
presence.

~

Deeper faith always provokes a searching need to
know God more closely. And one sign of this is
the presence of questions that rise up in the soul.
Often they have no final answer. They return periodically to the soul, disguising themselves in countless ways, never allowing an answer to settle a
matter once and for all. The question that Saint
Peter heard in the Gospel of Saint Matthew is an
example—". . . but who do *you* say that I am?"
(Mt 16:15). We may think at first that it is possible to answer this question all at once by affirming
the divinity of Jesus Christ as the Son of God. We
forget that the consequence of that answer, when
it is an answer of love, will draw further questions
and a lifelong quest to uncover the face of God in
Jesus Christ. The question Jesus addressed to Peter
was not a catechism question, nor is it to us. Little
demand for self-giving may follow from a mere catechism answer to Jesus' question. Even now, when
we hear his question, our response must be utterly

personal or it has little value. And only when our answer is truly personal does it open floodgates to new demands of sacrifice and self-offering from our life. Mother Teresa pondered precisely this question in a hospital bed in Los Angeles in June of 1983. She wrote a long meditation on "Who Is Jesus to Me?" Her answer concluded with many variations of Jesus' presence in the poor.

He is the Hungry—to be fed
. . . the Lonely—to be loved
. . . the Unwanted—to be wanted
. . . the Leper—to wash his wounds
. . . the Beggar—to give him a smile
. . . the Drunkard—to listen to him
. . . the Mentally Ill—to protect him
. . . the Drug Addict—to befriend him
. . . the Prostitute—to remove from danger

The answer is not surprising. A passion for God will inflame a passionate need to find his presence also in the poor.

~

It is always only some who see this truth of the poor with any interior vision. Those who do not experience it do not struggle to attain it. Spiritually, they may never go beyond a mere conventional approval of generosity to the poor. While they are perhaps charitable to the poor, the mystery of a real presence hiding in the poor never engages them in any search for the greater truth, which remains for them unknown. The concealment of Our Lord in the poor remains well protected because they do not seek to see him there. And they give no reply to what they cannot see. Often the repulsive appearance of a very poor man smothers in them any sharper response, which cannot thrive without a willingness to prostrate oneself in awareness of a long and terrible mistake. We have to admit our error with the poor if we are to discover the truth of the divine presence that the poor man offers us. Surely a grace is needed for that, a conversion that strikes a deeper chord of hunger in our soul. Then our vision will begin to change toward the poor.

~

The presence of God is never only in a church. Our Lord states clearly in Saint Matthew's Gospel that he will hide himself in poor people. "As you did it to one of the least of these my brethren, *you did it to me*." But now the desire for an encounter seems to shift somewhat. Often we may enter a church for a visit or for a more lengthy prayer seeking his presence in the Eucharist. Now, outside a church, it is God who seeks an encounter with us. In our contact with a poor person, a pursuit of our own soul is taking place, and we may not realize it. A conversion of insight is necessary to perceive this truth and accustom ourselves to it. Even if we ignore his presence there and do not perceive it, even if we are blind to this presence of Christ in the poor, the presence of God in these encounters is real. He does not require our recognition in order to be immediately present, as the Gospel of Saint Matthew makes quite clear. Our own choice to help or to ignore a poor person does not determine the reality of Christ's presence. The divine gesture of offering himself to us in the poor and, shockingly, begging from us occurs sometimes in spite of ourselves. He takes the lead in this and simply waits for our recognition. Often in our lives, as our faith advances after a conversion, we may sense that we are being pursued by his desire to be known. He wants us to unmask the poor man, rough and dirty, and perceive the invisible truth of his own presence in the moment. How often this happens we can scarcely know. Perhaps it takes place at times precisely as we are on our way to a church looking to find his silent presence in the quiet tranquility of the tabernacle. But we must first encounter him in the poor man if we want to sense his presence more strongly in the tabernacle.

∼

The continuing leap of a soul in giving itself to
God may be spurred on by events that are reveal-
ing quite transparently the desires of God. God can
always speak quite directly through events when a
soul is ready to hear. We have only to pay attention,
and then these events spark other forms of conversion that radically affect the course of life. An example comes to mind. At Christmas in 1996, while
in Kolkata, I visited Mr. Michael Gomez, then in
his early eighties, who was the owner and landlord
of a building where the top floor in 1950 served as
the first convent Mother Teresa used for her newly
formed order of the Missionaries of Charity. During the conversation, he told this story. It was the
spring of 1952, and the top floor space was becoming overcrowded with sisters. Mother Teresa knew
that she would need a larger location soon. One
day she asked Michael Gomez to accompany her
to look at a building on the outskirts of Kolkata
in order to have his opinion of its quality. They
had to travel by train, and as they passed together
through the entryway of the Harrah train station in
Kolkata, there was a sickly old man on the ground,
leaning on the wall with his back against the stone
entrance. They both noticed him, but they were
late for their train and passed into the crowds inside
the station. After completing their business, they
returned in the late afternoon. Mother Teresa now
approached the same old man, who had slumped

over against the wall. She bent down, grasped his
arm, and then cupped his face in her hands to look
in his face. Still squatting, she turned to Michael
Gomez and said that he had died. She walked back
into the station, returning shortly with a constable.
As the two walked home now through the crowded
streets, Michael Gomez related how upset Mother
Teresa was, almost to tears. How terrible that a
person should die in such a manner, she repeated,
with people coming and going, not noticing a man
dying. What a terrible, lonely way to die. It was
only weeks later that she picked up a woman eaten
by rats from a Kolkata street and carried her to a
hospital, refusing to leave if the woman was not
admitted. By her own account, after leaving the
hospital, Mother Teresa encountered more dying
people that day on the streets, and she went to the
municipality seeking a location where she might
care for such people. Quickly she was given an
empty building adjacent to the Hindu temple of
Kali in Kolkata. The unoccupied property became
her Kalighat home for dying destitutes, a work emblematic in her congregation and dear to her personally. The intense desire of a soul to give all to
God may find its mysterious counterpart in God's
desire to place a soul in the clear light of his will,
often by means of a poor man's presence.

～

Jesus went to pray in deserted places after he had
healed and cured disease and deformities. What was
the content of his prayer in those hours? Was it a
prayer of thanksgiving to his Father for these miraculous interventions in poor lives? This may be, but
perhaps there was a more mysterious reflection. His
oneness with the Father would suggest that a different inner experience overwhelmed him after those
miracles. A suffering combined with a great compassion may have overtaken him. The close contact with the crippled, the deformed, those marred
by disability and disease, surely overwhelmed him.
But another experience may have affected him in
a unique way. We forget sometimes that Jesus as
God is the Creator who is now one with human
flesh. Deformity and illness are a sign of something
gone awry in the creation. They are a consequence
of original sin. After these miracles, Jesus perhaps
suffered in the realization of the wound to creation
inflicted by sin and now manifest in the scourges
of disease and human disfigurement. He could not
simply look upon this wounding of the creation
with detachment. These solitary hours of prayer
after the miraculous healings were perhaps a preparation for the act of identification with the poor of
all time that he would make prior to his Passion.
His words in Saint Matthew's Gospel—"as you did
it to one of the least of these my brethren, you did
it to me"—find their anticipation in the miracu-

lous touch he exercised upon the poor in the years of his public life and express a concern that consumed his solitary heart in prayer afterward.

～

It would almost seem that there is a natural inclination in the depths of the soul to become poor. It seems to be there in the soul in a hidden manner. Perhaps this inclination to becoming poor is related to an awareness of mortality, which provokes in the soul a self-emptying impulse. In every society, one can find the vagabond soul, dirty, unkempt, disdainful of conventional life, stripped down to a ragged nothingness before eyes of the world. We commonly consider these people the marginalized, the misfits, and often they suffer from mental illness. Do such souls, however, unwittingly live a premature anticipation of every soul's poverty at the dark moment of personal dying? And have they been led by some deeper tendency in the human soul, springing forth in some cases from their mental collapse, to embrace a longing for that ultimate emptying of a passing selfhood that is accumulated in this life? Perhaps there is a lesson here. The poverty of the soul before its final moments is not something to leave for the end of life.

～

A Missionary of Charity Sister recounted that after
many years working for the poor, mostly in Brazil,
her vision changed one day. She was in charge of a
soup kitchen run by the sisters in Rio de Janeiro,
where about 250 men from the streets were served
a meal each day. The men who came were typically
drug addicts, rough in manner, worn and unclean,
aggressive at times with each other. Fights were
not infrequent, even soon after the few minutes
of prayer together before eating. One day a man
asked this Sister if he could speak with her before
he left. He had the wasted, dissolute appearance of
a man using drugs, and she expected perhaps a request for some favor or for some extra food to take
with him. Outside the building in a courtyard, he
quietly spoke to her. "You will find it hard to hear
this, Sister, but I am telling you because I want you
to pray for me. I am a *priest*. I was working with
drug addicts for a few years, and out of curiosity
I gave myself a taste one day, just to see what held
them so consumed and captive. One taste led to
another, and now you see what I have become. I
do the same things for money that we all do here,
but I won't say more. Please pray for me every day,
for my soul, because already it seems too late for
me." The Sister promised her prayers, but she also
recounted how deeply saddened she was, her heart
breaking at the sight of this man with a hard face
and in filthy clothes, and yet still bearing the per-

manent mark of the priesthood on his soul. She said she understood that day the concealment of Jesus in the poor with a new awareness of the reality. The existence of a sacred presence hiding beneath a distressing appearance came alive in her soul. It inflamed her faith in the reality of Jesus' presence in the poor with a concrete conviction it had not previously had.

∼

What is quickly forgotten is not for that reason unimportant to God. This may be especially so in omissions toward the poor. They leave a mark on our soul, often for a reason we understand only later or perhaps only at a final judgment. Every turning aside from a poor person remains with us even if the contact is momentary. It can happen even by a glance at the picture of a suffering child from a distant country as a newspaper page is turned and soon forgotten. Even such brushing up against misery can touch our soul in a certain manner. And perhaps we realize this when the same face returns on a different day some years later, older now, more stricken, jarring our soul even as we cannot recall who it is we are seeing again, perhaps giving us some chance to amend what we earlier ignored.

∼

We need to attend to what is most real in passing time, to resist leaning away in imaginative distraction from the present moment. Otherwise, we have no availability to God and may miss what he is asking of us. The losses can be irretrievable in a certain sense, never brought back in gratitude to a time of prayer. Moreover, God's requests have a way of hiding within small choices, especially in what can be done in kindness to a poor person. Perhaps he shows his face more frequently there than in the silences of prayer. But there is a discipline of spirit needed to immerse ourselves fully in the present moment and its opportunities for love. Only then do we sometimes catch God's eyes suddenly looking at us through the eyes of a poor man in what a moment before seemed to be an unimportant choice.

~

When close relations with God in prayer seem for a time blocked, and he is no longer so near and familiar, we should be ready, outside prayer, for a poor man to confirm Our Lord's companionship. A poor man stopping us just after we depart from prayer in a church and speaking directly to us is a sign of the constancy of God's closeness. But we have to have faith to recognize the divine presence in this sign. We have to adjust ourselves at that moment to the different manner of communication. We may prefer the setting of silent prayer for God's communications, but it is for God to choose how he will speak to us. A different quality of faith is necessary in the different encounter with his divine presence. The quiet presence of mystery in a tabernacle may be more congenial to our habits of faith. On the other hand, our encounter with the poor man offers us a chance to give immediate delight to the heart of God. We must simply believe that he is hiding in that voice and in that face. And then we must respond in action to a request that conceals the presence of God within it.

~

What is the effect on us, and on our prayer, if we begin to sense the mystery of God present in the poor and later lose contact with the poor? In neglecting or ignoring the poor, do we lose something of God as well? If we are attentive, we might observe that the link is a real one. A careless and cold approach to prayer may have its beginning on the day we tire of the poor getting in our way and then turn our eyes away from them. The presence of God cannot be fragmented. We cannot seek him in prayer in front of a crucifix or kneeling in front of a tabernacle and then ignore him prostrate and defeated on the ragged edges of this world. Sometimes a conversion of this kind is needed long after we have had a conversion from serious sin.

~

The "little ones" mentioned in the Gospel may be souls who have strayed into grave sin but have not rejected God in any explicit manner. An adventurous tendency of soul has carried them beyond boundaries they should never have crossed. But in the depth of their souls, they do not embrace an explicit malice against God. In that sense, the strayed soul is different from the soul that has taken a deliberate stance of rejecting God. This difference might be remembered because it may be present in the divine awareness of souls. In God's eyes, a person caught up even for long periods in serious sin can be both lost and yet still remain a "little one". He has fallen prey to his own weakness and is trapped. He is in trouble and needs to be rescued. The Lord is in pursuit of such poor souls. A sign of their true condition is that these souls remain attracted to goodness. Anything good and holy does not repel them. On the contrary, they often respect holy and sacred things when they encounter them. They retain a layer of innocence in their souls in spite of their sins. And it seems that the Lord sometimes shows great compassion in taking care of these souls. There is a mysterious indulgence of mercy offered to them, an exoneration extended to them beyond juridical standards, as though responsibility for their sins stretched beyond their own lives. No surprise, then, that the reference to "little ones" in the Gospel speaks of a harsh retribution for those who have initiated them into sins. And perhaps this is why they remain little ones, because their innocence was stolen, and why they receive a special mercy from God despite their sins.

~

At some point in life, if we are to love with greater intensity, perhaps we must settle on a primary intercession for which we will offer prayer and sacrifice. A category of souls in need must be chosen. The selection may not be our own to make; rather, it likely comes from God's invitation, if we have read properly the signs of divine providence. God will lead us to some encounter with a soul in need that is a taste of the affliction or risk facing a countless number of similar souls. Perhaps the starkest example is to confront a dying person who will permit no mention of God or prayer or sacraments. If we have been even once with a dying person who literally spits upon any mention of God, and nothing we say, however gentle and inviting, can overcome that frightening wall and barrier, we may walk away in utter pain, realizing that we must carry a soul now in prayer before God. A burden has been placed on our heart, and only callousness can ignore it. But what of so many others dying today and in danger of losing their soul without a turn to God's mercy? An intercession for souls on their deathbed in need of grace can attract us suddenly with its significance and remain a lifelong daily prayer.

~

There is probably no priest who is not given such a realization, usually rather quickly in his priesthood. In the early days of the disease of AIDS, when death came swiftly, before medications were found to control it, the mother of a young man in his twenties asked me to visit her son, who was dying of the disease. My appearance at the bedroom door in the parents' South Bronx apartment shocked the man and unleashed an ugly fury of venomous curses, first at me, then at his poor mother standing beside me. "Get him out of here, get that trash out!" A few words on my part only added oil to the flame. I departed for the sake of his sobbing mother. I tried another visit but again provoked the same dreadful reaction. The funeral was not long after, perhaps two weeks. No one but the two parents attended, alone in the front pew, with a handful of funeral home employees in the back of the church. A mother and father in the front row of an empty church who clung tightly to each other during the Mass and later wept uncontrollably as I prayed the Church's prayers of committal at the burial. I have never forgotten the fierce look of that young man rising up from one elbow in his bed, cursing with hatred in his eyes, or the tears of that mother and father as we rode back from the cemetery. And who can say how many deaths have repeated this pattern in the years since that week? Prayers for the dying in need of a final grace of mercy became an intercession for me from that day onward.

8

The Import of a "Second Conversion"

You must begin by an interior act, a little squeeze of the trigger, by which you abandon yourself entirely into the hands of Our Lord.

—Jacques Maritain to Yves Simon

Yield yourself fully to God, and you will find out! . . . I am speaking, of course, of great-souled individuals who keep nothing back for themselves.

—Saint Jane Frances de Chantal

What concerns me no longer concerns me; I must be from now on entirely to God and only to God. Never for myself.

—Saint Bernadette

It is not common, perhaps, to realize that the most significant conversion in our lives can come when we are already living virtuously, as it were. This is a conversion of the soul itself as we open ourselves to a more serious response of love in our relations with God. There are untapped layers in the soul that awaken only as we leap across boundaries in offering ourselves fully to God. New depths come alive in our interior soul once we place ourselves unreservedly in the hands of God. This form of conversion is primarily due to an attraction in prayer to give ourselves completely to God. Before this time, that possibility had the appeal of a beautiful ideal. Now the soul plunges ahead, resisting hesitation and any fear, casting itself into God and changing forever as a result. It is a true conversion of the heart and soul. A person now belongs to God, and the Lord is free to use a life in whatever manner he desires.

The explicit idea of a "second conversion" in the spiritual life was first broached by a Jesuit in the 1600s, Father Louis Lallemant, a novice master in France to one of the future North American martyrs, Saint Jean de Brébeuf. It is likely that he taught his young Jesuit novices the need to cross the threshold of a "second conversion" if serious holiness was to be attained. His view was that a man must come to a point in life, sometime after a commitment to God is already firmly in place, in which he realizes that he has not yet fully offered his life to God. Despite what may be years of faithfulness in a vocation, a deeper offering still awaits the soul. A life may be committed and devout and externally dutiful, but it still awaits a deeper realization of an entire offering of itself as an utterly personal act before God. A man has to arrive at a decisive reckoning in which he sees now with fresh eyes what it means to give himself unreservedly to God. Until that time, a life still lacks one thing, as Jesus says to the rich young man in Saint Matthew's Gospel. A man has not surrendered himself as yet in a complete offering to God. An utterly personal prayer of absolute oblation before God is still needed, which from the day it is made changes forever a soul's relationship with Jesus Christ. The act is a deep interior release of the soul to be from then onward at the complete disposal of God's purposes. In the setting of the 1600s and Jesuit missionary endeavors, Father Lallemant may have pointed to a readiness to face martyrdom as a test for crossing this threshold of the second conversion. And, in fact, the Jesuit martyrs of North America as a group did offer themselves to martyrdom prior to their deaths in upstate New York and Canada.

~

The notion of a necessary "second conversion" in a life already faithfully committed is striking in many ways. Father Lallemant suggests that without crossing this threshold, we pursue a lesser spiritual path and perhaps never think that there is anything more in spiritual life. This lesser path would not mean a fraudulent or compromised life, but it would signify a certain blindness regarding the purer demand of love that God addresses to a soul seeking him earnestly. The common idea of faithfulness as the high ideal of the spiritual life finds itself challenged here. As important as faithfulness is, discharging duty and maintaining a commitment do not satisfy God as much as we may think. There is a deeper interior dimension in a personal love for Our Lord that awaits our soul and that we do not realize initially. We have to sense an invitation after a certain point in life to risk everything and even life itself by means of a free, unconstrained offering to God. Only then, perhaps, can God truly do as he wants with us, with no question or objection from our part. Otherwise, the effort of love tends to settle down into paced and manageable generosity, undergoing the same aging and stiffening with the years as our body. The pursuit of the finer depth of love is missed, which demands the courage to offer ourselves unreservedly for the sake of a greater love that still awaits us. Once this is done in a concrete act, a new vista suddenly rises up in front of a soul, seized now by the attraction of unlimited self-offering.

～

A concealed tension of soul is likely present for some time before such a deeper *spiritual* conversion takes place. Without this tautness and strain at unseen layers of the soul, it would not occur.

This form of conversion is not directed at particular sins but demands, rather, a surrender of the soul that has been withheld to this point in life. Perhaps in most lives, the need for it has not been recognized, even while burning the soul internally for some time. The tension intensifies with the lack of recognition. In prayer, for instance, there may be a vague sense that crucial words are being neglected, that some important petition to God is being ignored. The soul feels a hunger for giving something to God, but what this might be remains unknown, unidentified in any concrete manner. What is God asking, if he is asking anything? What is it one must do? Nothing external in our life offers a solution. After a while, prayer itself seems to heap scorn on our soul for failing to find an answer, for not listening more intently. Or the reproach shifts to a frustration with God's silence, and our soul flails at itself in the quiet of prayer. In the midst of this unrest and perplexity, the thought may come that none of these difficulties has anything to do with an external decision. And then, if we are fortunate in responding to grace, our soul will give up the search for an answer located in external affairs. For a time, an uncertainty may seem to breathe in the air of prayer until finally we come to an interior crossroads. An urge is felt in a single hour to cast the unknown future of our life into the hands of God, to make an offering of the days and years stretching across the horizon beyond view. What God may do with this act of abandonment is his to decide. For now, all that matters is simply to entrust our life to him in a blind act of surrender. This step of courage is surely the one thing God asks from us at certain junctures in life. And indeed all along in life, this surrender of ourselves in ever deeper acts is what God is perpetually seeking from us.

~

The surrender to God in a "second conversion" requires an essential component. Without this element, a lapse into mere sentiment is possible, even likely. In short, we must be willing to suffer for love, with all the unknown days of our life still in front of us. The surrender is a great "yes" pronounced with absolute determination, a "yes" to giving the *entirety* of ourselves, including all the unforeseen and uncertain turns a life can take. The depth and intensity of that "yes" even to suffering is the measure of our soul's surrender to God. And, indeed, that willingness to hold back nothing in the offering of ourselves to Our Lord's love is a dramatic step spiritually. Do we know the day it takes place? Perhaps not; it may be carving itself into the deeper desire of our soul for some time. What we do know is that there is no surrender of this sort unless a life has become courageous and bold in love. For some time, surely, before such an act of surrender is truly present, a question repeats itself within the recesses of a soul, like a faint wind heard from inside a cave: "Will you lay down your life for me?" (Jn 13:38). The answer must be an offering spoken from the same depth within the soul: "Yes, I am ready, I am unafraid; I will love you at any cost." The words do not invite suffering into one's life; generosity, yes, and greater selfless-ness. We do not ask for suffering with this "yes", which would be a foolish and risky presumption. The "yes" rouses, instead, a great release from self that accompanies every intense love. It does not create new pain in life; it simply offers the soul to greater love. Every other question, even of suffer-ing, becomes secondary and is no reason for fear.

~

Perhaps a premonition of untold risk and danger accompanies a spiritual conversion of this sort. And this is what makes it difficult, the unknown con-sequences of a full surrender to God catching hold of the imagination, the fear of getting lost with no chance of recovering the familiar road, not know-ing beforehand what God may do, what new de-mands will ensue. Not knowing, it seems, if this surrender will bring our soul closer to God. And yet how could it not? Surrender to God from a deeper layer of soul always conceals a promise that must also be heard, even without words. God is not casual and nonchalant when great offerings are made. He does not receive them so frequently that he can be dispassionate toward a soul that casts itself in abandonment into his hands. His fingers are strong in holding on tightly to such souls. If these souls are asked to bear their share of suffering in future days after their offering, even so, the firm hand of God never releases them but, rather, clasps them to his heart. And that embrace compensates for every risk that might earlier have intimidated a soul.

~

A surrender of this nature may have a hint of anticipation earlier in a life. When Saint John of the Cross was escaping from his prison cell in Toledo after an eight-month incarceration, he made use of some knotted blankets tied to a window in order to drop down on a moonless night to the ledge of a stone wall. When he had lowered himself to the full length of the tied blankets, he found his feet still dangling; he was unable to get a footing on the stone wall and unable to see in the darkness. A miscalculation after releasing his grip on the blanket would plunge him down a steep precipice to his death. But he let go of his grip that night and landed safely upon the ledge of the wall. Surrender to God is much like this release in great trust into the hands of someone else's protection. The fear of finally letting go into the hands of another must be subdued and conquered if we are to cross a threshold of deeper relations with God.

~

The surrender of the second conversion has another element. Before it takes place, in a kind of concealed preparation, the Virgin Mary for some time quietly attracts a soul to this act. She is very intent to draw souls to an offering of their *entire* lives while the future of those lives is still unknown. This fearless casting of our life into the hands of God, inviting him to use it as an offering, can only be undertaken from a great love. It seems that Mary searches for souls who are poor in their desires, stripped down in their need before God, and who want nothing so much at a certain point of their lives as to make a great offering of love. She recognizes them because she sees in them the longing she possessed in an immense way at the time of the Annunciation—the desire to give everything of oneself to God. What Mary wants for these souls is that they awaken to the beauty of her surrender at that hour, which she expressed in her *fiat*—"I am the handmaid of the Lord; let it be to me according to your word" (Lk 1:38). She wants these words to seize a soul with a longing for the same act. Perhaps her words on that morning in Nazareth must be savored for a long time in our prayer if we are to take this spiritual leap in prayer into the "second conversion". For Mary, this act of her *fiat* abandoned her life entirely to God and already anticipated the complete gift of herself. In themselves, the words are the finest expression of a complete and fearless gift of a soul to God. Mary would like to teach souls their deeper import. The "yes" of her *fiat* placed her already in union with God, aligned the future of her life already in oneness with God's desires, and it can be so with us. Although we can only imitate and follow her, we cross a threshold of permanent transformation when this act begins to occupy our own prayer and even obsess it to some extent. The initial desire to make these words our own is already preparing us for the leap into the "second conversion".

~

God is always harder to love when his invitation to a greater love hovers around an eye darkened with fear. It is no surprise, then, that every desire for a great offering to God has within it a hidden grace not to fear. The act cannot be undertaken without a leap into unknown possibilities, and this dark prospect can intimidate. We can never see ahead what God may do with a total surrender of our soul to him. And God sometimes does ask much from a soul that loves him much. It is not surprising, then, that the act may provoke an anxious hesitation before it is fully embraced. Perhaps it takes much time and many tentative acts before we finally let go of a protective grip on ourselves and cast ourselves more completely into what can seem the abyss of God's uncertain hold. Although there may be an initial fear of this act of total surrender, the question should be raised whether anyone who became holy ever regretted a complete surrender to God. Surely the saints in heaven would testify that this offering took them to a depth of closeness to Our Lord that they had not known previously. They were free henceforth to listen to him more subtly and receive from him the endless stream of his requests for love and sacrificial offering.

∼

On the day I was ordained to the priesthood, a single statement remained engraved in my memory. Now, years later, I realize it was a hint of the great offering that must be chosen repeatedly in life. The statement did not come from the homily of John Cardinal O'Connor, nor was it any words of my loving parents. After the ordination Mass at Saint Patrick's Cathedral in New York City and a

period of blessings at side altars, I ventured outside to the sidewalk to find a ride to the seminary
in Yonkers, where a luncheon would take place.
An older New York priest in his seventies, stocky
and short, walked up briskly toward me with his
hand extended. I expected a congratulations and a
request for a first blessing. He took my hand and
gripped it tightly and pulled me down toward himself as he spoke words that have been etched for
years now in my memory. "You have just given
yourself entirely to God. Now don't spend the rest
of your life taking that back." Nothing more, and
then he walked away. I am still grateful to hear
those words repeated. But they have a different
meaning now, years later. An entire offering is a
demand whose magnitude I did not see until much
later in time.

～

The immediate effect of a "second conversion" in
the spiritual life is an interior disposition of soul
and a different quality of prayer—before this conversion expresses itself in acts. The "second conversion" fosters a *state of obedience* within the soul,
not just obedient responses in action. The surrender of a soul to God, the deep truth of belonging to
him, permeates the interior life because prayer has
found a home in this abandonment of self to God.
What may have been formerly a hard effort to sub-

mit ourselves to the hand of God, a struggle to pro-
nounce an interior "yes, I accept", or "yes I will
do it", has now taken on an ease of receptivity to
God's wishes whenever they are known. And these
wishes are more readily known because there is little resistance any longer to God. Our soul awaits
his request and command with a certain hidden
longing. It is like a devoted family servant of many
years who holds his employer in high esteem and
admiration and who longs for every summons into
his presence for some service, small or great. His
state of obedience is an availability that is constant
and never resented. Nothing is an imposition, and
all is understood, even when costly, as a chance
once more to love. Our soul will manifest a similar quality, but far more exquisitely.

～

In Saint Matthew's Gospel, Jesus compares the
kingdom of God to a merchant who finds a magnificent pearl and then sells all he has to buy it. The
image invokes the passion for God that can take
hold of us when we are ready to give all for him
alone and to desire nothing more than him. But
the parable may also quietly hide another truth. It
is not only we who can discover a treasure in God
that remains lifelong and consuming. Something
similar but on an infinite scale may take place in

the heart of God. When a soul turns fully to him in a consecration of itself to him, in a complete offering to him, God may look upon this soul now as if *he* has discovered the pearl he was looking for and waiting to find. God has no need to buy that pearl. At that point, it has already been given to him. But, instead, he will strip and divest that soul of everything that might cling to it so that it can be a pearl of great value only all for him. He makes of it a greater treasure when the soul has finally opened fully to him and belongs wholly to him.

~

A sign of crossing the threshold into the "second conversion" may be the sudden realization that it is the *crucified* Lord who dwells within our soul. Before that time, we may be aware of his indwelling as an article of faith that we acknowledge in our prayer of silence. But this new realization goes beyond the simple knowledge in faith that he dwells mysteriously in the hidden depth of our soul. We now encounter his presence within us in a more personal manner, with a great sense of his closeness, and for a very particular reason. We sense with a deep, intuitive certitude that he is inviting us to a special friendship we have not as yet known. There is one condition necessary—we must offer ourselves to his crucified love. The souls that do so will find that they cannot look at him anymore without the wounds of his crucifixion before their souls. The wounds begin to speak a language of love in the silence of prayer. They beckon us to offer ourselves for the sake of others, to surrender in prayer to unknown costs, all out of love. We must pass through these wounds of our crucified Lord into his heart's request and do so repeatedly. It is as though during our whole life Jesus Christ has been waiting for us finally to make this discovery. The souls that make this offering of themselves find a great release as a result. Their prayer is now drawn to a disposition of self-offering for others present in the silence of their hearts.

~

It is one thing to know in faith that Our Lord resides within us in the divine indwelling, inviting us to seek his companionship. It is quite another to awaken suddenly to the actual claim of Jesus Christ upon our life within our interior heart. We realize that we can have no deeper part in him, no real closeness, unless we allow his wounds to penetrate our interior soul. This is the invitation he is offering in the divine indwelling. It is a way of seeing the Cross, not as an external burden imposed on our life, but now, differently, as a truth inseparable from internal longings to let our life be offered more fully. The blessing is an immense one, like all gifts that accompany a soul's love for God. We finally understand that the "yes" to being wounded ourselves for love of him opens us into a mysterious intimacy with him. In affirming our "yes" to him, we know that this act delights him in a personal manner, because he has found another soul willing to share his Passion. This acceptance of a union with the crucified Lord within our own soul takes all suffering in life and transforms it into an exchanged gift of love.

~

The days following a truly wholehearted offering to God in prayer may seem to bring unsteadiness to our soul, as though our focus had become blurred and we were unsure how to direct our gaze at daily life. But perhaps this experience is simply show-ing us that we are now closer to having nothing other than God to draw our greater passion of soul. When we offer ourselves fully to God, mundane life can appear momentarily unreal and without sig-nificance, not worth the effort of our attention. But this is a passing disposition, and it should not be indulged with anxiety. Perhaps the important task then is a simple one. Our gaze needs to turn to the nearest person to reacquaint ourselves with the rea-son for offering ourselves to God with greater pas-sion. No offering to God is real unless our soul quickly finds other souls for whom we must offer our lives. We have offered ourselves to God, not to escape from life, but to plunge more deeply into life's true significance, which is always to realize the necessity of living for souls.

~

The "second conversion" is invoked when Jesus at the Last Supper tells the apostles that they are no longer servants, but he calls them now his friends. The difference is a shift from a more external relation to an internal bond of unlimited depth. The friend has not just a work to carry out, but an unlimited access to the heart of his Lord, and he will share in the desires residing in the heart of his friend, who is God himself. The friend will remain a servant in a certain sense because there is much to do always in service. But this work is never service in a strict or narrow sense of the term. The friend has been appointed to a work of intense love that will bear fruit and last into eternity. And for this he has to share in the divine friend's thirst for souls. He has to remember constantly that the thirst of our Lord became most intense as he concluded his sacrificial offering on the Cross. The friendship with Our Lord after a "second conversion" is an invitation to share his thirst for souls, a never-ending yearning to join sacrificially in an offering for souls.

9

Priests: A Need for Interior Conversion?

It has always impressed me that even his risen body was scarred with the wounds of the crucifixion. I cannot imagine an unscarred priest, a priest without wounds, because I cannot imagine an unscarred Christ.

—John Cardinal O'Connor

In the absence of deep inner life, a priest will imperceptibly turn into an office clerk . . . just solving daily problems.

—Karol Wojtyła

These are the chains that Our Lord has given to you. You must kiss your chains. Let yourself be overworked and devoured to the very limit. . . . Don't even think of changing your life, of leaving your post.

—Dom Florent Miège
to Jacques Maritain

Every priest should realize the importance of making a second great offering of his life to Jesus Christ crucified. Otherwise, he risks living out his life largely taken up with an external understanding of the priesthood. The first priests were martyrs. The end of these lives declares to every priest the essential challenge. A serious sacrificial pouring out of ourselves is the demand of love in this sacred vocation. But this pouring out is not something simply external and completed in service to others. The great offering of a priest must take place in the silent truth of his prayer. The conversion of priests is linked always to a renewed dedication to the life of prayer. A priest is a man of serious prayer and sacrificially committed to prayer, or else he is to some extent false and spurious despite his performance of holy functions. The priests who will not go a day without an hour in silence before a tabernacle seem always to be the vibrant, faithful priests carrying a love for souls in their own souls.

We are living now in a time when the priesthood and more radical forms of religious life ought to attract souls of holy rebellion. These souls exist in every generation, but in some periods of the Church's history they figure more prominently. Their emergence in any era is a testimony that despite appearances the intensity of faith at the core of the Church progresses over time. In most cases, the nature of such a rebellion is a fundamentally quiet one, drawing no great notice. But it has a com-

mon root in a deep aversion toward religious compromise. And this is the result of the crucifixion
of Jesus Christ carving a lasting discomfort in the
hearts and souls of some men and women. Calvary
hounds and harasses such souls. But it also draws
them to an intense gaze. They are not afraid to face
Christ's Passion and its challenge to their own lives.
The Passion of Christ is a recurrent provocation,
shaping the personal zeal of these lives and ani-
mating their desire for serious prayer. As a result,
while becoming priests and religious, they rebel
against an image of worldliness in the priesthood
and religious life that they find bloodless and bar-
ren. They refuse, sometimes at great cost, to follow
the fashions and passing trends. They oppose the
ordinary and largely unquestioned expectation of
clerical and religious compromise. They will not
accept a bourgeois priesthood or a comfortable religious life. In many cases, they are fools for Christ
and continue in time the wonderful tradition of
holy absurdity in embracing a crucified God.

~

One strand within the priesthood, by contrast,
seems to display a similar weakness in every generation—men who never adopt a spirit of heroic
independence in the pursuit of holiness. There
can be no holiness in any life without a serious

commitment to prayer. Priests ought to consider the self-contradiction of a priestly life without a search for deeper prayer. Yet it may be difficult to recognize inasmuch as it involves an interior truth, and the appearance can seem otherwise. Priests who pray only minimally may be steady, dutiful, moral men, often admirable in the help they give to others. But if there is no private passion for God in the interior of their souls, these same men tend perhaps to be insensitive to the disappearance of God in other lives. The presence of *souls* surrounding them may not touch them. The unbelief hiding in people, their anxious doubts and darkness, the lonely hunger in souls estranged from the Church, all this may not sufficiently alarm them. These priests may have enough of God to satisfy their own need, and their busy lives distract them. They serve the Church, but at the same time they do not spiritually inspire as they might were they to pray more. Perhaps it is more these priests, and not simply unfaithful priests, who are the reason why any era fails to attract souls to Christ.

~

Unfortunately, an inner disquiet taints the lives of many priests. Surely it has a link to prayer treated largely as the fulfillment of an obligation. The practice of prayers dutifully said, with no great desire for God, ends up tarnishing what should be a most sacred dimension in these souls. In every priest and religious, God exchanged a personal secret earlier in their lives, an invitation to a special depth of relations, unknown but to themselves, a secret that must be protected at the risk of obscuring the essential truth of their lives. Mere faithfulness to obligatory prayer is not sufficient to keep the flame of this secret exchanged with God alive and burning in a soul. Time alone in silence before a tabernacle is needed. The temptation to consider oneself too occupied to find such time is not uncommon. But when there is nothing for God in a day other than obligatory prayer, such prayer is looked upon to some extent as a burden. It is inevitable that a priest then starts to address God impersonally, and soon the real harm begins. Impersonal speech in prayer is a cold language. In some ways it is better to say nothing to God than to speak cold words, which over time will accustom the soul to a distance from God. Words rushed and repetitively recited, words without some receptive silence to listen to God, do not touch the soul, and neither, surely, do they touch the heart of God. The result is unease in a soul and an absence of a deeper spiritual longing. A soul has no deeper silence within it. And this is why priests are sometimes so restlessly active and scattered in their exterior activities. The absence felt in the soul because God is no longer so

personal is a painful reality even when unacknowledged—precisely because these same souls once
heard a voice of invitation inside their souls and
now they may feel some emptiness. They try to
assuage this dissatisfaction in activity or some type
of accomplishment that will be recognized, often
not realizing why they are driven in this manner.

~

The lack of attraction in priests for prayer is surely a
sign of distracted lives, sometimes too tired to pursue this difficult interior dimension of life. Yet the
absence of time spent in silence before a tabernacle, seeking the sacred presence of God, if it really
is a form of disinterest or neglect, implies a choice
to remain on the outer crust of religious pursuit.
It is one of the self-contradictions of clerical and
religious lives—to profess a solemn commitment
to God while forsaking the pursuit of close relations with God. This loss is akin to the tragedy of
a loveless marriage, with nothing more than occa-
sional small talk interrupting the more deafening
absence of communication—the silence of people
trapped in company they find tedious and at times
barely tolerable.

~

Tradition-minded priests who have little prayer beyond the claim of their breviary have little right to a frustration with Catholics who ignore a serious moral doctrine such as the ban on artificial birth control. It is true that the priest who prays his breviary observes the ecclesial law and fulfills his duty. In contrast, the Catholic couple who practice contraception engages in an objectively sinful practice. And the latter perhaps adopt a dismissive attitude toward authority in the Church. Yet the observant priest and the lax Catholic couple are linked by a parallel negligence. The priest may consider that he meets the demands of law in his recitation of the breviary. But a priest who completes in prayer only a legal requirement and finds no time for private prayer lives astride a rationalization not so dissimilar to the justifications that motivate violations of morality among married laity. In both cases, there is a failure of sacrifice. For prayer requires sacrificial choices and a sacrificial life-style. Only a man truly seeking God and the good of souls will treat this commitment with a sacred sense. More appealing activities can be pursued in work, and then of course there are recreations. Indeed, the priest who would upbraid the married man and woman for lacking a spirit of sacrifice when he gives himself only to rushed routines in prayer would not seem far from deserving Our Lord's stern rebuke to the Gospel Pharisees.

~

Spiritual illusion can easily occur if we concentrate too exclusively on performing well in an exterior fashion, in a style of preaching, for instance, with the thought that we stand before the eyes of others as our judge. The end result can be work that purports to be done for God and at the service of the Church and that seems to reflect a strength that must be of God. But where is a soul's awareness of poverty in this, its desperate need at times for divine help? Without poverty experienced in our life, and in our prayer, our sense of strength has become our deception, and the works we do as priests may retain their pride. We can know this because they leave little mark on others. So much done visibly in the Church is futile in the supernatural realm because no serious prayer lies behind it.

~

The parish priest unconcerned about prayer might say that his availability to people is the essential demand of his vocation. It is easy, however, to confuse social contact with people with a spiritual concern for them. Real apostolic zeal is certainly different. It is preoccupied with the presence of *souls* in the course of a day. This kind of awareness can only be due to a more serious approach to prayer.

Unfortunately, many priests treat prayer almost as an interference with the work of a day. A parish priest without much prayer tends to identify his life's work in measurable terms. Statistics, attendance records, collection counts, numbers served confirm his sense of service. But the danger of the eternal loss of souls in his care, including *all* those living within the boundaries of his parish, may not preoccupy him at all. In contrast, for a prayerful priest, the danger of Catholic souls long away from the Church's sacraments seems to be always a lingering obsession in his thoughts. It is why a priest's love for the confessional is a mark of his soul, precisely to catch such souls for Christ. Yet many priests seem to consider this a boring task and give minimal attention and time to making the sacrament available. Prayerfulness would awaken a different sensitivity, a spiritual anxiety for souls. Sadly, there is often nothing of the sort in a priest. Such a priest fails as a spiritual father to the wide spectrum of people entrusted to him by God.

~

We might as priests consider at times the possibility that a "spiritual work" attracts because of the recognition it will bring if successfully completed, and we might consider as well that a demonic temptation can sometimes hover in a dark corner of these inspirations. It is easy to seek one's own glory, and religion has always provided fine opportunities. It may even be at times that success-ful works of a religious nature cause more rejoicing in the underworld than in heaven. But of course that means there was a large dose of human van-ity to get them started and a spiritual fruitlessness at their completion. Often enough in the Church there are appealing projects that disguise spiritual emptiness behind gloss and a glittering façade, but only temporarily. Religious values may seem at first to be advanced in them, but there is a fraudulent quality, like a used car that looked so fine shining in the lot. Eventually it may be observed that human pride permeated these works. They are unfruitful and do not remain, and one reason for this is that they were undertaken in order to achieve a success that will be noticed and praised. In this respect, these works are hardly different from any venture at success in the world. In the spiritual realm, the cisterns that leak are very often those carefully con-structed by an element of human egoism. And they have no real prayer behind them. When we pray more seriously as priests, we are granted a deeper appreciation for humble efforts and hidden works for souls.

∼

While still young and searching in life, I met a man who after leaving the Catholic priesthood took a position in a vacuum cleaner company, eventually rising to a high executive status in the business. He attributed his success in life to what he called, if I remember correctly, the science of cybernetics. In that brief meeting, he showed a great passion for this pseudoscience of cybernetics. He said it had given him a clear direction as to how to advance in his life and find security and contentment. His love for his company was also very evident. Certainly when we parted, there was much unknown to me about his life. The conversation, however, was disturbing, even if my own Catholic faith was weak at that time, after hearing that he had abandoned the priesthood. Now, as I look back on it, this encounter was a grace for my life and offered an insight, which is surely why I still remember it. The hungers of the soul are easily interchangeable and transferable. And one can gain in the exchange, not a whole world, but quite truly a handful of dust.

~

The pursuit of any form of "success" in religion begs the question what we hope to achieve. What will accompany "successes" in the realm of religion and faith? In particular, the notion of "success" in the priesthood may hide a mild form of betrayal, a turning away from spiritual efforts for souls, gradual and then intensified, replaced over time by a need to be recognized or simply loved, a loss of spiritual purpose in many priestly lives that is never recovered. It is a remarkable phenomenon how many men who in youthful desire want to give their lives entirely to God in the priesthood end up with the same passion for vain reputation that can provoke worldly men to intensive activity in their various endeavors. We are not called to be successful, said Mother Teresa, but to be faithful. Faithfulness in the priesthood has one ultimate goal, which is to seek the salvation and sanctification of souls. Nothing else really matters, and all external appearances of ineffectiveness or even of failure mean nothing if a priestly life is fruitful in bringing souls home to God.

~

The saints teach us to mortify worldly motives and desire God alone and his glory. This cannot be ignored. And it cannot mean simply turning away from all that would entice us with illicit pleasure or satisfy ambition. It must mean also a refusal to be willful, possessive, calculating in doing good. Concealed in much of the activity we carry out as priests for the benefit of others may be a desire at times to satisfy ourselves and to enjoy our achievement or recognition. This, too, needs at times a spirit of conversion. The result can be "good works" and sometimes the accolades or appreciation of others. But the vitiated quality of willful good works, with their underlying strain of subtle egoism, is not difficult to notice. A disposition to aggressive action is often present, a need to succeed, a compulsive insistence to force our view upon others, to have our own way at all costs. These dispositions cannot be what God wants to see in priests, and they need conversion. Indeed, they spoil whatever good may be accomplished in action. And this means that they will produce only temporary fruits at best and no lasting influence for the good of other souls. The corrective is to remember always the need as priests to be empty of ourselves, as far as we are able, as we go forth from prayer. Our prayer itself must be full of a real poverty and dependency on God. Work done for God must be swept forward by his hand, and always with awareness that we do not always see ahead what he may desire to accomplish for the good of souls. We are small instruments who must be servants above all for the sake of souls.

～

Some years ago an Italian priest died at a summer beach outing for his parish after saving five children and two adults from drowning in the Adriatic Sea after the waves from a summer storm began to throw them against a rocky breakwater. The priest swam out repeatedly and helped each of them to shore. Crawling exhausted out of the water, his last words were to ask if all the children were safe. Then his heart gave way, and he expired. Fortunate, indeed, is a priest who finishes his life in an hour of intense love. But fortunate, too, are priests when they realize that the gift of their lives for others is the sole purpose of their life. The realization must burn each morning in silent prayer as a priest begins his day.

~

As priests, we can be more alert, more watchful, of encounters with unknown souls we meet for the first time, who even after a first contact can remind us how irreducible to chance are the random moments in a day. In some cases, the significance of these encounters is simply too obvious and pronounced to be a mere coincidence. We discover this truth in time as such souls become more deeply part of our lives. If so, something very often should be carried beyond that moment of a first encounter, above all the sense of a unique destiny that just passed before our eyes. Even the quiet observations we have of people convey something mysterious. The precarious uncertainty of a human life heading day by day toward a revelation of its eternal destiny may be largely missed. Are we not meant to foster and anticipate this implicit search in souls for God by recognizing the sacred presence of a unique truth in others as God sees them? Are we not meant to carry these souls back into a silent hour of intercession in prayer for them?

∽

The drama of grace has its moments. Some years ago a New York auxiliary bishop known for his zeal and prayerfulness was stopped by a thief at gunpoint on a street in the South Bronx and gave up his wallet. The young man asked him roughly, "What would you think if I shot you?" The bishop responded that he would be very happy finally to go to heaven. "And would you like to come with me one day?" asked the bishop. The young thief stared at the bishop without answering and then slowly sat down on the sidewalk, looking up at the crucifix dangling from the bishop's neck and gazing in the bishop's face. The two remained in silence for a time. Some minutes later, the bishop, about to impart a blessing, began the sign of the cross, but then stopped in the middle of his blessing, unable to recall what happened that he now held the weapon in his raised right hand.

∽

A priest has to have courage to persevere in exposing the truth of human sinfulness. It is a hard
duty surely to repeat with some constancy the need
for conversion and a basic sorrow for sin, and it
can be easily neglected. Almost all priests would
rather comfort than sound alarms. It can seem indeed an awkward impertinence to remind others
of sin when one is a sinner oneself, even if this is
done as gently as possible. But the priest who is
serious in prayer will discover that some of his spiritual passions are not for him to select and choose.
They are given to him within a context of the actual lives he serves as a priest. He cannot disregard
them without emptying his priesthood of an essential element of his service to souls. There is a
prophetic dimension in this vocation of the priesthood, and it demands a hard struggle in the realm
of truth. He has to respond with courage to the
challenge, or else he betrays his vocation. Yet only
those who are serious in prayer will do so—alone
as they are bound to become to some extent if
they discharge this duty with a true priestly heart.
For some priests, it may be their most difficult suffering.

~

Spiritual cowardice has always been available in remaining close to the crowd. While Jesus was being
crucified, the apostles kept their distance, huddled

safely behind locked doors. They may have whispered together angrily of Judas' betrayal, recalling
the signs they missed of his treacherous character, which now were clear. Perhaps one or two
in louder tones made plans for revenge, unaware
that Judas had already taken his life. Others perhaps pondered escape and a secret return to Galilee,
mixing with the Passover pilgrims at the end of the
feast. Still others no doubt remained quiet, trying
to tame a paralyzing fear. How different these men
soon became when Jesus showed his wounds to
them on the first Easter night. One by one they
became shocked and startled men, but astonished
also by a radiant light in Jesus' presence that they
had not seen to this degree before. A brief taste of
their later courage surely swept through that room
on Easter night, lingering after the risen Jesus disappeared. Even before Pentecost, they were changed
men, simply by seeing Jesus alive and bearing his
wounds. In looking on those wounds, which trans-
fixed them, they may have had a quiet, obscure
awareness of dying one day for what they had just
seen.

IO

The Witness of Simplicity

The apostasy of the modern age rests on the disappearance of the verification of faith in the life of Christians.
— Joseph Ratzinger

God does not consider what one gives, but what one keeps.
— Saint Ambrose

Don't you see that you have lost what you did not give?
— Saint Augustine

The words of Saint Paul that Jesus Christ, who was rich, became poor for love of us should pierce the heart after a conversion. These words point ultimately to the crucifixion at Calvary, where Jesus the poor man suffered ignominy and shame. A conversion of any depth can never be simply the correction of unsavory human behaviors. The encounter with Jesus Christ on a Cross, which may draw our first repentant tears, lingers in its impact on our soul. The impossibility of a life of excessive ease and comfort is the

187

consequence. A crossroad is faced in that awareness. Conversions will stumble or be waylaid entirely if we refuse to recognize the face of Christ as a poor man inviting poverty to some extent into our own lives. This challenge of simplifying our lives accompanies every genuine conversion. At the very least, Our Lord seems always to ask a greater generosity to the poor. The impulse to give away will affirm the truth of a real encounter with Christ in a conversion.

It should not be surprising that a desire for a simpler life-style is a common impulse after a serious conversion. This is not just the result of new discipline. The shock of finding God in a personal encounter, and of being known to him, is a penetrating light cast upon life itself. Standing before eternity, so to speak, is a jolting experience and awakens a realization that so many gratifications sought in this life are empty and unworthy. The awareness of time catches hold of our soul with a keen sense of the transiency and impermanence of the things of this life. What a year earlier might have been a coveted object to possess, a desire or ambition to be pursued, seems now unmasked for its paltry insignificance. It is truly as though a light from heaven had shone on the worldly pleasures and gratifications that formerly occupied our life with hardly a thought. This stripping away of the gloss and sheen covering much of life is a kind of revelation to the soul. The emptiness of the pursuit of self-gratification is soon tasted and often leaves a lasting aversion to indulgent habits in life. It is not surprising, then, that we turn to a different source of satisfaction. The life of prayer begins to attract us more. A kind of disinterest in chasing after chimeras roots itself in the soul. The result in part is the greater simplicity of life-style seen after every deeper conversion.

~

Although sin entails at times expensive habits, a self-centered life can be lived quite well on a low budget. In either case, a serious conversion confronts a soul with the need to overcome wasteful tendencies. A more sensitive use of money naturally follows. It bodes well for a conversion when a person senses the need not to spend money frivolously and begins to look for ways to donate extra money to the poor. But there is also a supernatural instinct at work here. The more deeply our soul has been affected by Our Lord suffering on the Cross, the more wasteful the spending of money can appear. Frivolous consumption and unnecessary purchases quickly acquire an unsatisfying and even bitter taste of emptiness. This time after a serious conversion is a ripe moment for an intuition. Jesus referred to it when he promised in Bethany, six days before his death, that the poor will always be with you. The words were spoken immediately after Mary of Bethany poured out her costly nard on him. The extravagance of her act included breaking that jar of nard, which the Gospel of Saint Mark includes as a detail in the scene. The gesture invokes a complete renunciation for a greater love, a release from worldly vanity, the casting away forever of a former life. "The poor you always have with you" (Jn 12:8). Those words will seek a mysterious pathway into every heart after a serious conversion.

~

There is a link between the crisis of unbelief in Western culture and the loss of religious intensity among those who claim the importance of faith. Belief is never simply an interior conviction about religious matters. It entails a personal cleaving to Jesus Christ as God and man that cannot be unaffected by his manner of life. But do we forget to keep our eyes fastened on the poor and crucified man of Nazareth whom we proclaim as divine and the object of our love? Belief in Jesus of Nazareth as God in the flesh has to face with some pain and distress the poor life he preferred for himself and the love for poor people that he chose. Otherwise, our faith in the Incarnation risks becoming an abstraction only useful for maintaining a correct belief. It misses an essential truth of his actual thirty-three years that calls for some effort of resemblance on our part.

~

To someone shocked by a first encounter with Jesus Christ in the Gospels, the absence of a simpler life-style in Christ's followers must be disconcerting. The thought may arise that a religion proclaiming the truth of God born of a poor virgin in a manger, a God in human flesh who remained in lifelong poverty and who died naked and crucified in an appalling Roman execution, would require an emphatic rejection of worldly riches among its adherents. Vain indulgence in pleasure and worldly pursuit would seem an insult to the image of Jesus presented in the Gospel pages. Perhaps there are followers of Christ who are embarrassed by this incongruity. Yet if the objection is raised, it tends to be quickly dismissed under some rubric of the human joys that sustain perseverance in Christian faith. It is a serious challenge, however, to set our mind on what God might reply and not fall back on easy human interpretations. The profession of Christian faith verges on a self-contradiction without a denial of excessive material comforts. More than we

think, it may be that people outside the Church ask
whether the conviction of many Christians conceals indifference toward the crucified God whom
they have not yet managed to disavow. If so, it is
a strong incitement to souls after a conversion to
live a genuine effort at simplicity in their personal
lives as a countermeasure to this perception.

～

It has always been true in Christianity that an effort
to find some workable balance between a sacred
and a secular outlook produces internal conflicts in
a soul. Unfortunately, what is initially experienced
as an inner conflict often shifts in time to a choice
for compromise and accommodation. The necessity of worldly pursuits triumphs in many lives,
while the search for the sacred diminishes in importance, taking on a smaller portion of life. The
result is not inconsequential. The pursuit of a plea-
surable, more enjoyable life of accumulated riches
in this world has the inevitable cost of neglecting a
deeper, unmet need of the human soul. And linked
to that loss is usually a failure to bear witness to religious truth and to a personal encounter with God.
The difficulty of a rich man to enter the kingdom
of heaven, as Jesus insists, is preceded in the Gospel
by the story of the young man with many posses-
sions, who cannot take up the offer to give to the

poor and follow Our Lord. This story is emblematic of an essential conflict repeated countless times in human lives.

~

If Jesus of Nazareth, our Lord and God, gave himself to the death described in the Gospels, how is it that a disquiet does not register somewhere in the peaceful soul of someone who kneels head bowed before a crucifix after receiving Holy Communion at a Saturday evening vigil Mass and follows this act of piety in the next hour by an expensive meal, while a diseased child in sub-Sahara Africa sleeps restlessly in the long hours of this same night after finding nothing on a plate for dinner but the dust of a windswept desert?

~

We are all quietly implicated in the omissions that every materially comfortable life incurs toward the poor at any time in history. In this we forget that Christ at Calvary contemplated silently in his hours on the Cross the whole of history's indifference toward the poor of its present day. Indeed, the forgetfulness has repercussions beyond our own lives and that of the poor. It may be that there is a direct correlation between the crucifixion of Jesus Christ and the presence of the poor in any age. When the poor are ignored, when little thought of their suffering intrudes into other lives, the crucifixion itself as the central event in history is obscured. Callousness toward the one is an indifference to the other. We often hear the Jewish refrain not to forget the Shoah, the horror of the Nazi holocaust. Our own life-style and use of money ought to display evidence of a parallel memory. The presence of the poor especially in Third World suffering is the presence of the crucified Lord in mystery and disguise. The refusal to forget the link is to keep our eyes open to the perpetual reality of the crucified Jesus Christ in the current day.

~

Certainly it is a less noted phenomenon in the history of Christianity—the debasement of sacrifice and voluntary poverty as an esteemed value at various times in the Church. This loss of respect for sacrificial living during any era of the Church couples ordinarily with every crisis of faith in the Church, either as a preparation for it or as a symptom of it. The debauched lifestyle of pre-Reformation Churchmen is a classic example of the damage done to faith by habits of indulgent lifestyle. Always it is the case that less drawing power is felt toward the doctrinal claims of Christianity when renunciation and sacrifice are reluc-

tantly tolerated or even dismissed as spiritually irrelevant. In particular, when the general trend in
priestly and religious vocations is to cast off sacrifice in lifestyle and commitment, there is a di-
minishment among Catholics in their conviction
that the costs of adhering to the truths of Catholic
faith are not too high to pay. This unfortunate link
between the disregard for sacrifice and the crisis of
faith has been a pronounced phenomenon of our
own time.

~

Abbé Pierre, the French Capuchin founder of
the Emmaus "ragpickers" movement after World
War II, which joined poor people together in com-
munal living, was visiting New York City in 1983,
where a branch of his Emmaus movement had a
house for the poor in Harlem. The house was
a night shelter for the homeless, and I was living there as a volunteer at the time. During his
visit, he was invited to speak at Saint John the Divine Episcopal Cathedral near Columbia Univer-
sity. The cathedral was being renovated at the time,
and the outside of the massive building was cov-
ered all around with scaffolding. The venue for the
talk was informal, a fundraiser of sorts with drinks
and hors d'oeuvres in a large hall on the cathedral
property. The sizable crowd from the Episcopal
community were well-dressed and milling about

sipping cocktails when Abbé Pierre in his brown Capuchin habit was led to a stage and began his talk at the microphone. He did not speak English, and a translator stood beside him. Abbé Pierre was about seventy at the time, but still full of fire. His voice became fierce and lancing as he proceeded, while at his side the translator spoke in a very subdued monotone. This famous priest, who had worked in the French Resistance during World War II, began by saying that the previous night, on his way to use the hallway toilet, he had tripped in the dark over someone sleeping on the floor just outside the bathroom. It is true that there were often not enough beds for everyone in that house. He then asked, raising his voice a bit, whether anyone present who had a son or daughter sleeping in such fashion could tolerate this indignity. Would they not bring that son or daughter immediately home that very night? And how could so much money be spent, he chided with his voice rising, on the stone façade of a building when poor people suffer having nothing? His volume escalated as he pursued that theme; all the while the translator maintained his bland monotone. It did not take long before the first woman walked out in obvious displeasure, followed soon by many other men and women, so that the back door could not be exited without a delay. The rector of the cathedral stood near the door repeatedly apologizing, trying to be heard over the thundering voice of Abbé Pierre.

Whatever I might think now, at that time for me it was to step for an hour into a page of Jeremiah. This French priest may have been my first contact with a saint, and I wish not to forget the memory.

～

There seems to be perhaps at times a tendency among well-off and comfortable Catholics, when they encounter a family member showing some committed interest in the poor, to dismiss this as an eccentric inclination, tolerable as long as it is temporary, but necessary in time to outgrow. On the other hand, there are eras in the Church in which giving up societal favor and privilege for a life with the poor has been contagious. In the medieval period, Saint Francis of Assisi, Saint Clare, and Saint Thomas Aquinas are only single instances of this widespread pattern in the Franciscan and Dominican orders. Even in our own time, in the 1970s, 80s, and 90s, hundreds of Indian women, a certain portion from upper class backgrounds and a boarding-school education, joined Mother Teresa's congregation to give their lives to poverty and the poor. It would be opportune to see a phenomenon like this on a large scale happen again in this new century in the Church. What new congregation perhaps can draw the heroic attraction for voluntary sacrificial poverty from the young?

～

A paradox of the spiritual life evident for those who love the Eucharist is that every apparent loss we incur regarding worldly circumstance invites a gain in relationship with a God who offers himself to souls each day in the sacrificial immolation of the Eucharist. The divine providence by which God makes this truth known can be striking to those who have found a daily sustenance in the Eucharist. Daily communicants, from my observation and experience, do not succeed entirely in their ambitions of worldly success. There is always some intervention, some obstacle, that keeps their lives humbled. They are thwarted at one level only to awaken to a deeper richness of Our Lord offering his companionship in a personal way. The conversion of such lives takes place when they happily realize their protection from a pitfall of spiritual life, namely, to achieve fully what an element of pride in the soul identified as a prize. The beauty of receiving the Eucharist daily in itself simplifies for many people the needs of a life.

～

Real love for the poor requires more than the contribution of surplus monies, even with regular and generous habits. Allocations motivated by pity for the poor are noble and admirable, but they hardly answer to the demand of the Gospel to invite the poor into our lives. A donation from a safe distance is a glance in the direction of the poor. It may appease the pangs of a Christian conscience. But a donation is really only a response to a clear duty. For a rich man it is a way to avoid an omission that may be in fact judged with severity by God. Signing a check to alleviate the suffering of the poor is of course not a negligible act. It is a way to clarify our need for greater simplicity of life-style. But real love for the poor as described by the Gospel demands actual contact and touch, not distant gestures. In many cases, when Mother Teresa received in person a donation from a wealthy person, she thanked the benefactor, but then said she would be happier still if that same person would donate some time to work in one of her homes for the poor. And in some cases, like that of Tony Cointreau, inheritor of a family fortune from Cointreau liqueur, the invitation was accepted. He volunteered for many years in the Missionaries of Charity home for AIDS patients in New York City.

~

Dorothy Day was asked in 1949 by a group of Maryknoll seminarians on a visit to her Catholic Worker house for the poor in the Lower East Side in New York what she considered the gravest problem facing the Church in America. Her answer was the bourgeois materialism of the clergy, which she said would collapse the love and respect of American Catholics for their priests. And surely that was a time of much less clerical privilege in material comforts. But truths do not change, including practical truths. The reluctance of priests to adopt a poorer life-style is still a reason why priests do not inspire greater respect, even from Catholics strong in faith and disposed to accept the humanity of their priests. Distaste for living poorly deprives their lives of what could be an immediate appeal. Service to others is always admirable, but there is an intangible attraction when the life of a priest or religious has become poor and weary in self-giving, yet willingly relinquishes comfort, all the while remaining happy and content. People may indeed long for this witness from their priests as a reminder not to consume their energies on wasteful pursuits in their own lives.

~

Sacrifice and self-denial in priests when they are still young, a readiness for hardships common to the lives of the poor, is already a good prediction of the spiritual fruitfulness they may have in the Church. The sacrificial priest is invariably also a prayerful man. On the other hand, it is predictable as well that priests who become accustomed to excessive material comforts will undermine their desire for prayer and their capacity to leave any permanent mark on souls. More than a priest may consider, it can be an arduous effort to focus attention at Mass after hearing a Gospel about Pharisees and their love of money and not to think of the man at the pulpit who just recited these words.

~

The phenomenon of "cerebral orthodoxy" among priests is nothing new in the Church. It has long been on display on at least two notes: men committed to the teachings of the Church, doctrinally loyal, but at the same time enjoying lives of bourgeois advantages, concerned for money and higher class pleasures, keeping their lives far removed from contact with poor people; secondly, men zealous to uphold orthodox Catholic teaching, eloquent and sharp when presenting Catholic truth, but passionless in another sense—their knees have no time for prayer before a tabernacle. On both counts, often enough seen in tandem and in fact spiritually linked, there is a self-contradiction in the lives of these priests and complacency not easily corrected as long as the flagstaff of orthodoxy is raised and held in high esteem. Unfortunately, a priesthood of this type offers itself to a caricature—a kind of quasi-profession of men in the religion business indulging the privileges of an elite status—clerics in polished Roman collars clinging to their breviary with one hand, gripping credit cards and a check-book in the other.

~

It might be good to ask whether a weakness for worldly refinement and enjoyments is precisely why prayer becomes at best a mere obligation in many priestly lives. The attachment to the material satisfactions of good food and drink, costly entertainments, and tasteful surroundings is often hardly considered. These priests become dependent on these comforts, which may seem more necessary as their position in life advances. By contrast, a deeply prayerful commitment in a priest seems never to allow this kind of indulgence in worldly tastes. Sadly, more prominent positions in the Church seem always to bring increased material comforts. The link between the prestige of an appointment and obvious improvements in life-style is hardly questioned. One could call it almost a historical truth of Catholicism. Now the Church is hearing a different challenge. It would be a striking experiment with Pope Francis to see a reverse practice and a contradictory attitude being urged and even mandated, not least because it might be adopted by some in the hierarchy and passed along as an example to priests.

~

It is worth asking as well whether in the Church's history the saints of the poor have provoked far more conversions than the saints of the pulpit. When Saint Paul affirmed that he had not come with the persuasive force of worldly eloquence, he wore the poor, dusty clothes of a tentmaker. But why cannot a combination of these qualities be the mark of a love for the priesthood in the present day? There have always been priests of this character, and they are a hidden holiness in the Church. To preach from one's poverty, living also a life to some degree poor, teaching as much from one's outpouring of life as in words, is the great aspiration that can take hold of a priest's life. The presence together in a priest's soul of these qualities can be expected to draw a great fruitfulness for souls.

11

Love for the Eucharist

What does it profit you if Christ comes in the
flesh unless he also comes to your soul?

—Origen

God would never want to do other than give if
he found souls to whom he could give.

—Saint Teresa of Avila

When he gave me himself, he gave me back myself.

—Saint Bernard

*There is no deep conversion in a Catholic life without a
new perception of the Eucharist. The attraction for Our
Lord's presence is suddenly sharp and vivid when we place
ourselves near a tabernacle. Now we understand why the
Church speaks of the* real *presence in the Eucharist. We
experience the reality for ourselves in our proximity to him
inside a church. Our Lord gives a gift of himself and dis-
closes himself in this awakened experience of our faith.
The challenge is to keep a vibrant love for the Eucharist at*

the heart of our lives. Many people after a conversion begin to attend Mass every day, and the practice remains a life-long treasure. The discovery of Our Lord in a conversion becomes a continuing quest lived out day to day for deeper contact with him. The Eucharist is Jesus himself, and the need to remain never far from him is often implanted by grace in the depth of our soul at the very outset of a conversion. This favor is meant to be a permanent grace.

"Come to me, taste of me; stay with me, listen and learn from me." Jesus in the Eucharist summons us to himself in definite terms. The invitation may resound strongly after a serious conversion. Our Lord wants us close to him; he wants our desire near him. He wants us never to lose the allure of his presence in the Eucharist. Ultimately, he wants our union with him through the sacredness of the Eucharist. There is often a mysterious drawing attraction felt in the soul after a conversion, a *sursum corda*, an unmistakable longing of the heart when we place ourselves over time in physical proximity to the Blessed Sacrament. The person of Christ is a *real* presence when we are praying before a tabernacle. After a conversion, we may realize this truth as though for the first time. It is not simply the Sacrament that is known as a real presence. A veil lifts, and the personality of Our Lord becomes a real presence and is felt more deeply in a mysterious manner. His summons to "come to me" is sensed in a very personal manner. We can listen to him without hearing him speak. We can be aware of his unseen gaze. The desire to approach closer and stay in his presence rises up within the soul in the days and months after a conversion. This drawing power of love in the presence of the Eucharist can be keenly felt at times, or it may not be felt at all, and still something draws us to him in a tabernacle. In a deep conviction of what is unseen with our visible eye, we can know that we are inexplicably loved when we are in the physical presence of his invisible reality.

~

There is no real conviction in faith after a conversion without a desire to experience the *living* God in a personal manner. A deeper faith cannot but hunger for an experience of real contact with God's presence. The essential beauty of Catholic life is found here, in the accessibility of our God to the quest for a deepening personal encounter with him. The presence of Our Lord in the Eucharist offers the most immediate occasion for this direct encounter with God. His personal presence in a tabernacle, secretly communicating to us and compelling our attraction, is impossible to forget once it is known. Indeed, those who love prayer seem always to possess a mysterious attraction for the Eucharist. Catholic churches, especially in cities,

remain a perpetual testimony to this truth. Desire
for prayer and a longing for the Bodily Presence
of Our Lord become inseparable and indistinguish-
able needs. And yet we must recall that it is always
in the poverty of a small Host that Our Lord invites
our love and adoration. The disguise of poverty is
the common choice for the divine concealment in
our midst.

~

Anyone who begins after a conversion to pray with
regularity before a tabernacle or monstrance must
recall periodically that the Eucharist is not properly understood unless the actual, living Person of
Christ is the presence we seek in praying before
the Eucharist. The Blessed Sacrament can never
be described as the most sacred *thing* in one's life.
The Eucharist is not a thing, but the real personal
presence of someone who is in physical proximity
to us, even if not seen, wherever the Eucharist is
present. Properly speaking, the Host is not a sacred
and precious object, but the invisible presence of
Jesus Christ himself now in heaven concealed by
the sacramental sign. All prayer before the Blessed
Sacrament is an entry, an invitation, into this unseen reality of an actual personal presence. The reality of his presence lies beneath the appearance,
which only covers over and veils his presence in
the visible appearance of the Sacrament. For that

reason, prayer before a tabernacle or monstrance is not immediately comforting to our senses. We see a Host, and yet we are in the presence of our God in the flesh. If we find ourselves comforted, it is in the knowledge that he is there in the flesh. That knowledge is deeper to the extent that our faith is very personal in speaking to the hidden Lord present in the Eucharist.

~

The presence of the divine mystery in a Catholic church ought to include a regular remembrance that our attraction for the tabernacle is a gift for which we cannot be sufficiently grateful. The sacred allure of a tabernacle in a Church cannot be explained. The mystery of that attraction is never an easy comprehension. We simply know it and treasure it in an utterly personal manner. Our eyes gravitate in the direction of the tabernacle when all is quiet because someone is there in that location even as he is silent. The tabernacle is itself inseparable from the mystery of the divine presence in a Church. We sense in an utterly Catholic manner that this blessed location of the tabernacle is the secret hiding place for the sacred presence that it encloses. He summons us to himself there, and we find in a lifetime of prayer before the Blessed Sacrament his ever penetrating gaze.

~

There may be a need at times to overcome the abstract tendency of our mind when we are praying in the presence of the Eucharist. Small conversions are necessary to enter into a deeper faith while praying before the Eucharist. The real presence is the fullness of the incarnate Christ. In the Eucharist, the reality of Christ is in front of our eyes, the flesh and blood presence of Jesus himself in his sacred humanity, most starkly in an hour of Eucharistic exposition. But because we are blind and cannot see the actual reality, we may sometimes tend, without realizing it, to worship the Host as a sacred object in itself. The Host we see on the altar is sacred precisely as a mere appearance hiding the reality of human flesh and blood, the incarnate Son. We must step beyond the veil of appearance in the sacramental sign and address ourselves to Our Lord personally, even as he is concealed. Otherwise, our prayer in looking at the Host can be like staring at the clothes a man is wearing instead of gazing in love upon his face and speaking to him.

~

Absence of reverence by a priest toward the sacred mystery of the Eucharist is a gesture of untruth. Do priests pay sufficient attention to this? Lack of respect and awareness in the presence of the Eucharist is a way of casting doubt on the reality of the Sacrament. It has contributed to a loss of conviction among the laity toward the real presence of Christ in the Eucharist. The choice to maintain a devout manner, attentive to the sacred mystery, not as an external performance, but out of genuine love for the Eucharist, must be considered a demand of contemporary spiritual witness. It is a witness needed precisely before one's own Catholic brethren. And this is true for priests, religious, and laity.

~

The sacredness of the Mass itself is in the invisible action taking place. The traditional understanding is that every Mass is an unbroken identification between the priest's words of consecration at the altar and Jesus' words of consecration at the Last Supper and the actual pouring out of his blood on a Roman Cross. The three distinct events become one in the Mass. Perhaps we find ourselves vexed and exasperated when attending a Mass that is less than devout in the recitation of the words of consecration. We might remember that the long siege at Calvary was not a comforting sight, nor were the shouts and harsh voices. It is true that the ritual of the Mass is honored properly by a serious prayerfulness on the part of the priest. But the sacredness of the Mass is not constituted by the external performance. Even at Calvary, the sacrificial action, which is the essence of sacredness in the Mass, took place in a setting of enormous tension and disturbance.

~

In 1989, when John Cardinal O'Connor was Archbishop of New York, a group of homosexual agitators advertised a plan to disrupt his Sunday Mass at Saint Patrick's Cathedral. The police were alerted, and priests were invited to attend as a show of support for their bishop. The Mass was uneventful until after the Gospel was read. Then, as the cardinal began preaching, a few dozen men stood up from various seats of the vast cathedral and began shouting foul obscenities and ridicule in the direction of the cardinal. The cathedral echoed with the bristle of curses and contempt. The police quickly stepped in and began removing the men from pews while the congregation joined with the cardinal in praying a fervent Rosary. Some of these men, however, had chained themselves to the pews. The difficulty stretched the time to a lengthy interruption. Finally the Mass could continue. But some men had waited for another moment of verbal assault. As the consecration was prayed by the cardinal and a hundred or so priests in attendance, about six men from the protest now rose up from the pews in a resurgence of blasphemous abuse. The loud shouts were thick and crude as the sacred words of the consecration were recited by the united voices of the cardinal and his priests. I was in my first year as a priest. I left the cathedral that day with an entirely different understanding of the Mass and its actual mysterious link with the noise and filth that surrounded Jesus Christ hanging on a Cross outside the walls of Jerusalem.

~

As our life continues after a conversion, the Mass is only superficially lived if we do not place our own lives on the altar of sacrifice and reaffirm our own offering in union with Christ's offering. Mother Teresa asked many priests to remember her and her intentions when they placed the drop of water into the chalice of wine at the offertory. She wanted her own life and her intentions for souls to be mixed and united with the sacrificial offering. The need to do likewise with our life is imperative when we attend Mass devoutly. The Mass for those in attendance is not simply to be an attentive observance of the sacred action. It demands that we ourselves be drawn into the sacred offering of Christ himself. The Passion of Christ must be allowed entry into our own desires, so that we long for this offering with him at Mass. We are to be "given up" and "poured out", just as Christ himself is at each Mass.

~

Sadly, it can almost seem a choice by some priests to remain at the external surface of the extraordinary mystery when they are offering Mass. The words of consecration may be enunciated clearly, but at the same time they pour out at a quick, hurried clip. No hint of real mystery occurs, no slowing down to cross the threshold of a momentous instant. It can sound as though by pronouncing the consecration at a rapid pace, the priest is trying to avoid letting the sacrifice of Calvary leap beyond the paten and chalice into his own soul. And so we encounter at best the discipline of a liturgical act instead of the union of divinity and human nothingness that is possible when the Mass for the priest leaves his own soul momentarily naked and trembling before God.

~

The Eucharist is not a static reality, unmoving, a thing to be honored and admired like a painting in a museum. No, it is alive, like a fire burning and leaping with flame, never entirely still, an immolation that never ceases. The immolation takes place in a hidden manner, in ultimate mystery. It does not attract notice except by love and a deep faith. The One who offers himself in the sacrament of immolation wants our recognition of love, but this requires an effort on our part. For the sacrament of immolation is also the sacrament of self-effacement. If we begin to love this hidden offering always present before our blind eyes, it draws us, and we want a deeper union with it. The Eucharist is the sacrificial immolation of Our Lord, but always in a concealed way, and we must believe in an unseen action of infinite depth to be touched by his profound power of love. It burns away all dross of desire in those who draw closer to it. His purity pierces the soul. It consumes the shredded and cut pieces of our soul and unites them to him in love. The reception of him in Holy Communion becomes a kind of perpetually renewed consummation of a single consuming desire filling our life.

~

When we realize after a serious conversion the true holiness of the Eucharist, the presence of God himself in the Host, there is bound to be a spiritual discomfort and unease in seeing at times the dishonor accorded the sacredness of the Mass. Fervent prayer at Mass can be an arduous task when challenged by casual priestly gestures, slapdash improvisations, banal comments. With the rapid words and quick movements of some priests, it can be difficult to realize that an enormous event takes place with every consecration at Mass. The external displays are often hard to distinguish from an indifference to the transcendent mystery. The clerical disregard for the sacredness of the Mass, moreover, cannot be unlinked with a diminished faith in the real presence of the Eucharist among many Catholics. The almost universal reception of Holy Communion at weekend Masses raises precisely a question of real belief in the truth of the Eucharist. The phenomenon is a symptom of the privatization of faith in our time. Relations with God, including reception of the Eucharist, have become for many people a matter of private determination, without reference to a wider body of shared Catholic discipline and belief. The likely prevalence of sacrilegious Communion, with perhaps no comparable precedent in history, surely contributes in turn to a slow bleeding within the Body of the Church during the current era. The uncertain, vague sense of the Eucharist is aligned inevitably with a reduced awareness of the person of Jesus Christ as true God and man. A soul recently converted and drawn to the Eucharist will be sensitive to these signs of the times.

~

The wounds of Jesus on the Cross have vinegar poured upon them whenever a sacrilegious reception of Holy Communion takes place. Most people who receive Holy Communion in mortal sin may be oblivious to this hidden truth. They do not consider the terrible sacredness of the wounded body of Christ. Like the Roman soldiers, they do not realize what they are doing, but this lack of awareness is not without consequence. These souls become like many bystanders at Calvary, who may not have slung spittle and insult at Our Lord, but who wounded him badly by their lack of concern and compassion. Nothing in their hearts directed their eyes to linger on his torn and battered face at the crucifixion. In a similar way, it may be that souls who receive Holy Communion sacrilegiously are quite incapable of turning their thoughts to Jesus Christ suffering on a Cross. They consume the actual Body and Blood of the crucified Lord, perhaps seeking a spiritual comfort, and do not realize the wound they callously inflict on him. They are unaware that the Blood of Christ should soak into a soul in the reception of the Eucharist. When a soul is carrying unrepentant grave sin and receives the Eucharist, the Blood of Christ pours out as though on gravel and stone, spilling to the ground. It does not enter anything and is wasted. But this Blood is the actual person of Our Lord himself. A soul without realizing it keeps Our Lord from entering the deeper regions of its human life when receiving him in grave sin. Without an awareness of the sacredness of the Eucharist, the barriers to repentance may only harden in a soul.

～

The Eucharist is the sacrament of spiritual hunger.
We eat and then hunger for more. We receive an
intimate closeness with the Lord and desire still
more. We touch him and take him within our soul,
and yet it is not enough. We have him for moments
and wish to hold him always. He becomes our possession, and we long to be owned entirely by him.
He seems to wait upon our words, and we find
ourselves at times overcome by wordlessness. We
look up at a crucifix over an altar and then realize
after receiving him that his Passion is alive within
our soul. We ask him for oneness and union, and
he instructs us to thirst with his thirst for souls.
We turn to him in longing, and he seems only to
gaze at us. We hunger for him, and in return he
consumes our desire with himself. The sacrament
offers the most intense union with the mystery of
God in the flesh.

~

The reception of Holy Communion is not for the
comfort of the soul. That is too indulgent a view. It
has a deeper, hidden purpose that is generally not
considered. We receive in the Eucharist not just
the presence of Our Lord, but the presence of the
Passion of Jesus Christ crucified into our soul. We
are united to a body that still bears the marks of
a terrible suffering inflicted on it. The union is always with Jesus Christ *crucified*. We can never sep-

arate the reception of the Eucharist from a real encounter, an encounter by touch, with the wounds
of Our Lord. This union with him by means of
his crucified body and blood has a serious spiritual implication. The reception of the Eucharist is
meant to draw us closer to the sacrificial Passion
of Christ. We are to learn a mystery for our own
life by a proximity to his suffering. He wants us to
look at his wounds when we receive him. There
we will learn everything needed for love, which is
essentially sacrificial. The Eucharist is not meant
for comfort; it is meant to draw a soul to greater
sacrificial offering. It is the great sacrament of a desire compelling us to surrender fully to his Passion
living itself again in our life.

~

The inclination to sacrificial living is a "natural"
consequence of the frequent reception of the Eucharist. Converted souls in particular should understand this link between a greater closeness to
Our Lord in receiving him and the impulse to pour
out ourselves more generously in self-giving. We
are receiving a Lord who was sacrificially offered in
a complete way. This disposition to sacrifice which
was deep in Jesus Christ culminated in his final
sacrifice on the Cross at Calvary. The reception of
the Eucharist has the effect in a prayerful soul of

drawing forth a desire for our own sacrificial offering. Our soul senses that somehow over a lifetime we can be united to the passionate offering of
Christ himself. The sacrament compels a drive in
the soul to be enmeshed mysteriously with Christ's
sacrifice. And this will mean to share in his thirst
for souls on the Cross. The Eucharist seizes our
soul with this desire for souls by its very nature.

~

A Missionary of Charity sister recounted in Kolkata
that one morning at Mass some years ago in the
motherhouse of the congregation, a small thin Host
from the ciborium had dropped to the floor between the altar and the tabernacle. The breezes that
pass through the chapel in the winter months had
blown the consecrated Host from the filled vessel
during Communion time without the priest being
aware. A novice sweeping the chapel after Mass saw
the Host and told her mistress of novices, who then
informed Mother Teresa. The novice mistress said
that Mother Teresa made her usual genuflection
upon entering the chapel, approached behind the
altar, and then knelt in front of the Host on the floor
in adoration for a long time. She remained with her
head bowed in prayer, unmoving, her eyes down,
her hands folded. Many times in her life, Mother
Teresa repeated that the presence of Jesus Christ

in the Eucharist was inseparable from his presence concealed in the poor. The presence is one presence, she constantly affirmed. The same Jesus who hides in the Sacrament is disguised in the distressing appearance of the poor man. As she prayed on her knees before that Host in Kolkata, one wonders what may have passed through her heart and mind. In her saintly awareness, Jesus Christ on the floor of a chapel was the same Christ lying sick and abandoned on dirty street corners and alleyways throughout the world. Our love for the Eucharist can only deepen as we receive him in Mass only to go in search of him in his concealed presence among the poor. This truth can be a great provocation after a conversion. A rhythm of seeking and finding him in his real presence can extend outside the Mass to many unsuspected moments of a day if we open our eyes differently to the poor —in all their disguises of isolation.

12

Passion for God

Bury yourself with our Lord, lost, unknown. It is your vocation.

> —Abbé Huvelin to
> Charles de Foucauld

Gratuitousness in love leads to great poverty; and the greatest poverty is needed to be able to accompany Jesus crucified.

> —M.-D. Philippe, O.P.

Jesus Christ will be in agony until the end of the world. We must not sleep during that time.

> —Étienne Pascal

Every release from ourselves in giving ourselves more fully to God takes us more deeply into a passion for God as the ultimate love in our life. The initial experience of a serious conversion is a first release and has already the seeds of a great offering of our lives to God, if only we seek it. The struggle to say "yes" to God years earlier becomes over time a need to affirm the deepening "yes" of a complete

*surrender to God. The souls that follow that path of sur-
render to the end will come to many crossroads in which a
demand to seek God with pure desire and intention confronts them. The mystery of God in his love for the soul
may become more mysterious even as he is known in certitude as the beloved companion of our life. A passion for
God deepens, and perhaps it leaps into fire at times when
we realize the need for a further offering and surrender to
him. These acts of greater surrender in the course of life
amount to ongoing spiritual conversions. They take our
soul over and over again to a hiding place we cannot see beforehand and where he waits always in concealment for us.*

Whether, after a conversion, Our Lord truly becomes the *beloved* of our soul is significant beyond
measure and all-important in the life of prayer.
This, too, like an initial discovery of God, entails a necessary interior striving; it means we must
choose Our Lord as the beloved passion of our life
and then let prayer be affected by this choice. If he
becomes the beloved of our life in a quite determined manner, something resistant to fading and
decline will return always to grip us again with a
desire for prayer. The deeper layers of unfelt desire
in our soul will always continue to stir with some
unseen flame. We will seek with a passion of the
soul to meet him in prayer. We will belong to him
and know this as an ultimate truth of our soul because he is our *beloved*, and we want nothing else
but to belong to him.

~

Without this passion of the soul for Our Lord as our beloved, prayer can descend somewhat over time to an exercise in cold formalities, more like reading a book than meeting a real person much loved. And often, for men especially, prayer does not attract a deeper pursuit because Our Lord has not become the beloved of their soul, which often comes more easily to a woman in her prayer. Those who have not crossed this threshold have not yet come under the sway of a profound attraction in prayer, and they need another conversion in their life. It is never just the infinite mystery of divinity that makes prayer difficult. If we approach God with faith but without a great longing to know him as the beloved of our soul, we may never realize except vaguely his infinite desire for union with us. Even hidden from our eyes, he must be met with a passion of love. Crossing this spiritual threshold requires a conversion of our soul's deeper passion. And how to arrive personally at this conversion is an ultimate spiritual question. Our choice of him as our only beloved is the simple answer, difficult as that act may be. This act in itself, when it is deeply chosen, draws forth an insatiable yearning for him within our soul.

~

The initial conversion in the life of Charles de Foucauld had both a long preparation and a critical hour of denouement. After completely losing his Catholic faith in adolescence and living an immoral life as a young French officer in late-nineteenth-century North Africa, then returning to explore at serious personal risk these same desert lands as a cartographer, he went back to France all too aware of his inner emptiness as an unbeliever. The uncertainty and irresolution lasted for some time. In his own description, "there was a restlessness, an anguish in my soul, a desire for truth, and I used to pray over and over again, 'My God, if you exist, make me know You.'" Finally, with doubts and turmoil tormenting his soul, he was encouraged by his cousin to seek out a well-known confessor at the Cathedral of Notre Dame in Paris— the Abbé Henri Huvelin. On this decisive morning of his life, he approached the priest's confessional, where, in European style, the confessor sat open to view. Charles had already prepared what he was going to say, hoping for the priest's understanding. He said that he had not come to make a confession and that he did not believe, that he wished only to talk. The priest's reply was immediate: "Make your confession, and you will believe." We do not know if Charles de Foucauld hesitated or felt any chill in his heart or a strong urge to walk away. What we do know is that a moment later he was on his knees pouring out his many sins to a priest. At the conclusion of that confession, Abbé Huvelin asked him if he had eaten anything yet in the day. When Charles said no, he was instructed to receive Holy Communion at the next Mass in the cathedral. And that single hour in the Cathedral of Notre Dame transformed everything in his life, placing him from that hour forward on the path of an extraordinary passion for Our Lord, ending with his martyrdom in Algeria in 1916.

~

The approach of our soul to God as our *beloved* is decisive for our relationship with God after a conversion. It affects how our heart will seek him, whether we will have a passion for God and pursue him through every unknown turn and venture in life. We have to be confident in calling him the beloved and not hesitate in using such a word freely, or some variation of it. But this means that in truth he has seized a heart that has willingly surrendered itself to him. The surrender to him as our beloved must be repeated often, even on what may seem drab days of prayer. The surrender in itself purifies our soul. Unless we allow our desire for God to undergo purification by these repeated acts of surrender, we risk a halt on the path to God. If there is covetous desire or a self-seeking

motive in prayer, even as we seem to surrender to
him, he is not really our beloved. Our love for ourselves may be stronger. In that case, we still need to
empty ourselves in a greater generosity and purity
of intention. Any possessive impulse toward him,
even hidden and unnoticed, will confine our soul
to the periphery of love as long as this tendency is
not overcome. Conversions of our interior desire
in prayer are at times necessary. A deep purity in
seeking him must be sought frequently. In a kind
of conversion of our heart in prayer, moreover, we
must overcome a fear of ever losing him, which
sometimes accompanies a more intense purity of
desire for God. In the dark contemplation to which
Saint John of the Cross alludes, in the secrecy of
a blind longing for him, Our Lord must be firmly
known as the beloved one. For a soul with a passion
for God, his concealment never alters his identity
as the beloved, always sought and awaited.

~

Conversions of all types always have an immediate
effect on our prayer. God as the beloved compels
a need for personal encounter at the very heart of
prayer. He draws our soul to seek him. At first this
invitation seems to place him more open to view,
accessible to our conversation and our need. But
one of the more subtle effects soon experienced

after a conversion may be a first taste of the absolute holiness and transcendence of God. The taste will intensify as we are faithful in seeking God in the silence of prayer. The mystery of divine transcendence is inescapable in all deeper experiences of prayer. This truth is evident above all when we pray before the real presence of Our Lord in the Eucharist. For the gift of the Eucharist is what it hides—the concealed presence of Jesus himself. We have a blind man's eyes when we kneel before the Sacrament. Our blindness in gazing at the Host in a monstrance mirrors our mind's incomprehension when God in his mystery silences our thought. We do not *see* what we are looking at in the Host— the real presence of Our Lord in his resurrected body. Nor do we know what God may think or how he may react when we speak our heart to him in prayer. And yet we can be certain that he listens. His answer to us may exceed our capacity to hear it. Over time, if we pray seeking only God with a great purity of intention, we can sense that our incomprehension of him is above all an incapacity to realize how penetrating and pervading is his love for our soul.

~

Along with this sense of incomprehension, the humanity of Our Lord draws and touches us in the years after a conversion in an increasing way. We

might find ourselves one day asking, for example, why Jesus shed tears at the tomb of Lazarus.
He knew already before arriving in Bethany that
he was going to perform the miracle of restoring
Lazarus to life. He informed the apostles of his
intention before the journey from Galilee. Why,
then, these tears when he drew near the place of
burial? After first encountering Martha, he made
his way to the tomb of Lazarus, calling Mary, the
other sister, to come. Mary's arrival interrupted his
approach to the tomb. There she reproached Jesus
in words mingled with her own tears: "Lord, if you
had been here, my brother would not have died"
(Jn 11:32). The Jews around her were also seized
by emotion and shed tears. We are told that Jesus
was greatly disturbed and he wept. But what is the
reason for these tears? He knew what he intended
to do shortly; in the next minute he would be calling forth Lazarus from the tomb. There may be
indeed a reason for these tears that is rarely considered. Earlier, with Lazarus gravely sick, Mary
and Martha had sent a message to Jesus: "Lord, he
whom you love is ill" (Jn 11:3). The words are
starkly direct in their appeal to his love. Their very
simplicity suggests an absolute assurance found in
great prayers of intercession that all will be fine.
And who composed these words? No doubt it was
Mary of Bethany, who in Saint Luke's Gospel sat
at the feet of Jesus and listened in rapt attention
while Martha was occupied in the kitchen. The

words Jesus spoke on that day are often identified with his special regard for the contemplative vocation. "There is need of only one thing. Mary has chosen the better part, which will not be taken away from her" (Lk 10:42). Her experience of his personal love must have been very great after that contemplative hour with him. A deep confidence and trust ordinarily accompanies the knowledge that we are much loved. Probably it was unthinkable to Mary that her petition for Lazarus would not be heard. Yet in a shock to her soul, her later appeal for her brother was apparently ignored and Lazarus died despite the petition. In composing it, she may even have thought that Jesus would understand the words to mean as well that the one he loved who was ill was she herself, in grief at her brother's dire condition. This death of Lazarus must then have devastated the heart of Mary, but not just the death; rather, to brood depressingly on the fact that her request was not taken seriously and met deaf ears. A heavy disappointment, a conviction of a much lower place in Jesus' concerns, would have seized her. Her tears at the feet of Jesus near the tomb of Lazarus would have been the sorrow of a gravely disappointed woman, convinced that she had mistaken his love and meant much less to him. If this is true, the encounter by Jesus with the despairing emotion of Mary may in turn have caused a terrible wound to him, drawing from him the weeping recorded in the Gospel.

Perhaps we do not consider this possibility so read-ily in our reflection on this passage of the Gospel. In truth, Jesus may have wept from seeing a soul he especially loved now bent down in tears, refusing to look at him, cut off and withdrawn, because her request had not been answered to her expectation, even as he intended to fulfill it. Perhaps a flash of divine awareness in Jesus occurred at that hour for the many souls in the future who, in loss or tragedy, would indulge similar disappointments toward him and lose confidence in him because their expecta-tions would not be answered by God to their lik-ing. At the very hour when he is near and his love is the greater, we easily misperceive his timing and his manner of intervention. In Mary's case, we can assume the likelihood that she at least recognized her mistake and the wound she had caused to Jesus. Shortly afterward, a few days later, she poured her alabaster jar of costly nard over him in a gesture of total love. It is gestures of this kind, which are true hours of conversions, that may take a soul deep into a passion for God as an all-consuming need. And sometimes they come only after we realize the possibility of inflicting great pain upon the heart of Our Lord. The one who loves much is often the one who has realized a capacity to wound much the one who is loved.

~

The sooner our soul accepts that what God desires to give in prayer is a deeper encounter with his transcendent mystery, the more securely do we advance in a passion for God as our beloved Lord. There is a link between our passion for God and our experience of his ultimate mystery as God. This connection is especially true in contemplating Jesus Christ in our prayer, who as a man looking at us nonetheless conceals infinitude in his eyes. The face of Jesus in the Shroud of Turin can have this effect on us if we gaze at it with love for some time. Looking at this face in a lingering gaze, we confront a mystery beyond our conception. We are staring at our beloved God in the beaten face of a crucified man. The divine reality hides there in that mysterious face and we cannot surpass the limits of our human vision. And yet, strangely, as his face remains before our eyes, it contradicts any suggestion of an insurmountable barrier between our soul and God. His features, the closed eyes, the swollen cheek bones, the teeth clenched in death, draw our own passionate desire even as this face hides a presence of utmost mystery. We can only speak of an inexplicable conversion of soul in the experience of gazing on the face of the crucified Lord. It is as though his face had a mysterious power to overcome all our natural sense of separation and distance from God.

~

The transcendence of God in mystery means in part that we glimpse him only in small fragments of his infinite reality. For that reason, the hour of any encounter with God in prayer is always a bit deceptive. There is so much of him that remains veiled and hidden, enclosed behind impossible barriers of distance. It is easy to imagine at times that we have attained a more substantial grasp of his presence than is actually the case. We cannot "measure" God's presence by our own limited capacity to sense his presence. It is not just that there is always more beyond any immediate experience. We have no way to know how much more of an overwhelming reality of love is present even in the immediate hour. What do we receive, then, when we speak of an encounter with his divine presence? What can we answer but that he seems to lean down toward our soul and bend over it, until he is gazing at it from within our soul's inner depth? We can to some extent know this truth and experience it in prayer. But we also experience that in his coming to us, our capacity to make a return in love is overwhelmed. We can only desire and wait in desire. The closer he seems to be in his gaze of love, the more an inner desire seems to concentrate its longing for him without any effort. This experience draws forth our passion, not so much to know him, but to be overcome by him. Our soul longs for a complete surrender in love to him, and this in itself is an exquisite manner of knowing him. The knowledge of him is inseparable from the inner passion that draws us to him. He who is near draws forth our longing to be vanquished in love by him. What was at first a discomfort with his transcendence has become a longing to disappear within his transcendent mystery. The mystery at this hour has become a reality of love.

~

It cannot be temerity to aspire to a personal encounter with God. If we believe in him, then he must be sought with passion and with a confidence that he will be found. Otherwise, faith is emptied of an essential meaning. Perhaps greater temerity might do our soul great good after we have returned our life to God, provided it is refined over time. For inasmuch as we seek God with greater passion, he offers a more obscure experience of himself. No doubt over time he is asking for a change in our understanding of a real contact with his love. A conversion of awareness is necessary in prayer as we continue to seek God. It is an elusive encounter that is sought in a lifetime of prayer. Temerity is necessary for a life of deeper prayer in its surrender to divine love when it is not enjoyed, not possessed. And we cannot persevere in such a pursuit without a blind, cleaving faith in God's longing for our soul despite every sense of absence.

~

Many initially strong desires for God can become
fading vestiges of their original strength if hope
does not accompany these desires. This virtue is
critically important after a conversion in order to
sustain a lively perseverance in our desires for Our
Lord. It is our desire and passion for him that compel the steady offering of ourselves to him. This
is a fundamental truth of prayer. The dynamic of
prayer is largely an exercise of our passion for God
and the offering of ourselves that flows like an endless current of desire within our soul. The desire
to offer ourselves to God can remain unceasing
due to the nature of desire, which is to be in an
unfulfilled state. Dissatisfaction to some degree is
inseparable from the nature of being in a state of
desire. When we finally possess what we have de-
sired, we no longer yearn for it. But before that
time, our desire can only be sustained as we anticipate a fulfillment and possession in due time.
We yearn in desire for what remains yet beyond
our possession. And so hope must accompany our
desires for God to keep them burning with fresh
yearning. In souls alive with the grace of contemplative prayer, desire and hope weld together exactly in this manner. Hope is oil dropped upon a
flame within our desire for God, keeping it ever
burning.

~

Where does God lead souls that find no secure place in this world but into the desert of the heart? The desert within them is the secret destiny of these souls, not by their own design, but by a divine choice. They seem to find no permanence in any one place or in any lasting company. They belong to God alone, and he makes this divine choice evident to them. But for that realization, a conversion is necessary. They may live among crowds, enmeshed in activity, surrounded by noise, but their solitude belongs to God, and they have to accept it. When these souls discover the great attraction of solitude with God, usually after some years of struggle, their hearts are finally at peace. The solitary heart becomes for them an enclosure for God, and they are at last content. They have found the inner sanctum where, alone with God, they are never really alone. Interior solitude becomes a most welcome refuge, and it does not matter if God does not speak there. The silence has become a sacred companion in every hour of solitude. The solitude may be stark and bare, but a thirst for God is present in the silence. What they seek in silence is what all seekers of deeper prayer await—something akin to the whisper in the desert winds rolling along stretches of brush and sand, faint and rushing, then fading back again into silence. These whispers in silent prayer always leave an immense longing in the heart.

~

The offering of ourselves from a condition of empty distress is not at first a desirable act for any soul. Yet perhaps there is no greater expression of firm conviction in faith than to speak words to an unseen God from a place in the soul of inner darkness, not knowing by any sign or evidence whether this cry pierces the thick shadows and arrives at its destination. At some point, if we are serious in our pursuit of God, we need a spiritual conversion in this regard. We must be secretly convinced in such prayer that our few words have been heard by another and already are being answered within our soul. Prayer offered in darkness is a blind prayer, but in no way is this blindness equivalent to a disability of soul. Words of prayer spoken in blindness rise from a depth in the heart that is unavailable when we seem to be seeing so well. The blindness takes us to a deeper layer of soul and concentrates our longing in a single desire. We want only him, and nothing else that brushes the surface of our lives interferes with that desire. Even overcome by shadow and a grey malaise, our soul in blindness can be present to his presence. We have no help at that time but the conviction of his presence, but what else is needed? Unlike our own, his eyes are not blind, and we can know his gaze on our soul. And the few words spoken to him from the heart of that interior darkness take no time at all to pierce the heart of God.

~

If a person has undergone a serious spiritual conversion and is ready to offer all in life to God's choice, it should not be surprising that God takes that life into a greater solitude with himself. The common thought that being alone is a sign of misfortune gives way to the realization of an immense blessing in belonging only to God. The solitude in question is not just the disciplined provision of times set aside for prayer and for solitary endeavors. In this case, it is a realm of solitude in the actual life itself at the core and depth of our being. The soul perceives that it has made a kind of espousal with solitude because aloneness is necessary for a deep companionship with God. This realization does not mean that we are without friendship, even the friendship of marriage. But offering ourselves wholly to God radically alters our soul's personal relations with God. No other desire for a human bond can correspond to the longing for God that burns in this blessing. Again, the solitude that attracts the soul then is not a desire for isolation or withdrawal from human relations. It is, rather, a sense of depth, an abyss opened in the soul that, once tasted, attracts us to further offerings of ourselves to the only ultimate beloved of our life.

~

"Blessed is he who takes no offense at me" (Mt
11:6). The words of Jesus are his last message to
Saint John the Baptist, imprisoned in Herod's dun-
geon cell, awaiting an execution. They are a response to John's message sent to Jesus—"Are you
he who is to come, or shall we look for another?"
(Mt 11:3). John's question seems at first surprising.
He had identified Jesus earlier at the Jordan River
as the Lamb of God after baptizing him. Does he
no longer perceive in Jesus the presence of his Mes-
siah and Savior? No, it is more likely that he begs
for a confirmation of a truth that he still possesses
but clutches now painfully, given the turn of events
in his life. The truth of Jesus Christ has not disappeared from his soul, but thick layers of dark
shadow now encumber it. The turn of events and
his imprisonment weigh heavily on him, and in that
dank prison cell, John is perhaps the first to undergo what mystical writers will later call the dark
night of the soul. If so, involuntary, uncontrollable
questioning was tormenting his spirit, and he could
not chase away these thoughts. His abandonment
and loneliness, perhaps his inability to pray, left him
prey to whispers of making a great mistake. Had
all those years been an illusion, a trick and deceit,
at the expense now of his life? Did he miscalculate
in giving his life for nothing but an imagined

and false impression? Jesus' words to John are the answer to every serious trial of darkness a soul may face in life, because they are words of blessing. "Blessed are you when you are not offended, not plunged into tears, not devastated and disappointed, when I offer my Cross to you. Blessed are you when you perceive my Cross as a sign of special favor to you. Blessed are you when your time of darkness is united to my abandonment on the Cross. Blessed are you when you love me more intensely in the time of trial." For some souls, the greater their desire for God, the more reason they have to expect significant testing in the bitter taste of inexplicable darkness. These periods of testing are nothing less than the path to union with Jesus Christ crucified.

∼

We have to be careful perhaps not to remonstrate with God because he asks much of us. We are not his advisors; his designs and plans do not need our counsel. In this regard, we can recall Saint Peter interrupting Our Lord in Saint Matthew's Gospel when Jesus predicted his Passion and crucifixion. "This shall never happen to you" (Mt 16:22). Stay close to me, by my side, no one will ever harm you. The words are distressing when we know the three denials that soon await Peter. Unlike Peter, we do not object to Jesus' Passion, for that hour has been

completed. But perhaps we do propose removing
the Passion from *our* lives. Even without explicit
words, we would like Our Lord to remember at
times his divine omnipotence and his need to use
it. We are ready to instruct him on a better direction for events that may be causing us pain. We
may even rebuke him if we think he is careless and
remiss on our own behalf. In all this we forget that
the Passion is now ours to embrace; his Passion
is over. But this passion of ours, like that of Jesus
when Peter objected, likewise permits no rebuke
on our part toward Jesus. An effort to alter Our
Lord's choice, even worse, a refusal, can only draw
a grave retort, as it did for Peter. The words in our
own case, however, may be a bit different from
his words to Peter. Not "get behind me, Satan"
(Mt 16:23), as to Peter, but "are you able to drink
the chalice that I drink?" (Mk 10:38). If we are to
hear an ever greater summons to love throughout a
lifetime, we must say a "*yes*" to that chalice many
times in life. A loving hand with permanent nail
marks has extended it to us. Let us not refuse to
go far in our love for him who first has loved us.

~

It is a question that has confronted certain eras of
history: If Christianity was reprobated in society as
a crime and entailed a clear risk of denouncement

and possible imprisonment and even death, could I say after a conversion that I was living in such a manner that with each day I was opening myself to increasing suspicion and to the possibility of an imminent arrest? Praying the Creed at Mass may be symptomatic of a state of soul in this regard. Sometimes we should imagine we are pronouncing these words while standing next to a person who does not believe them, even in a church. The words can be recited in a kind of cold routine, barely holding our attention, in no manner drawing us. Yet to profess these words implies a willingness to die for them. Is this an exaggeration? A conversation in prayer with a contemporary martyr might alter our view. There has always been a final wordless article of the Creed expressing our readiness in fidelity to Christ to be scorned and despised and to prefer that our life be taken violently rather than renounce our love for Jesus Christ as our beloved Lord.

∽

In the present state of the world, Christianity *must* become a heroic Christianity

—Henri de Lubac, S.J.